DATE DUE

THE ROCK CARLING FELLOWSHIP

1976

The role of medicine

DREAM, MIRAGE,
OR NEMESIS?

THE ROCK CARLING FELLOWSHIP

1976

THE ROLE OF MEDICINE

DREAM, MIRAGE, OR NEMESIS?

Thomas McKeown

THE NUFFIELD
PROVINCIAL HOSPITALS TRUST
1976

Published by the
Nuffield Provincial Hospitals Trust
3 Prince Albert Road, London NW1 7SP

ISBN 0 900574 24 0
© Nuffield Provincial Hospitals Trust, 1976

Editorial Board
Lord Cohen of Birkenhead, CH, DSC, MD, FRCP
Sir Edgar Williams, CB, CBE, DSO, DL
Gordon McLachlan, CBE

Designed by Bernard Crossland
PRINTED IN GREAT BRITAIN BY
BURGESS & SON (ABINGDON) LTD
ABINGDON, OXFORDSHIRE

CONTENTS

vii

Contents

PREFACE

Speaking of the origin of an idea a historian once remarked: 'It is always earlier than you think'; and certainly it is not possible to name the sceptic who first questioned the effectiveness of medical procedures. But at least from the time of Montaigne, the notion that treatment of disease may be useless, unpleasant, and even dangerous, has been expressed frequently and vehemently, particularly in French literature. Molière's *Le Médecin Malgré Lui,* the famous operation in *Madame Bovary* and Proust's account of the psychiatrist's cursory examination of his mortally ill grandmother ('Madame, you will be well on the day when you realize that you are no longer ill. . . . Submit to the honour of being called a neurotic. You belong to that great family . . . to which we are indebted for all the greatest things we know) are examples of the irony and bitterness with which some of the greatest writers have expressed their conclusions about the work of doctors.

Remarkably, considering the eminence of the critics, such views have had little effect on medicine or the public's estimate of it. Perhaps they were not meant to be taken quite seriously; indeed Proust wrote: 'To believe in medicine would be the height of folly, if not to believe in it were not greater folly still, for from this mass of errors there have emerged in the course of time many truths.' Or possibly, being expressed humorously, the criticism incurred the risk of being considered frivolous; it is at least arguable that Shaw's lively Preface to *The Doctor's Dilemma* had less influence than the Webbs' seriously worded essay on a public medical service in *The Report of the Poor Law Commission.* Whatever the explanation, until recently the contribution of medicine to prevention of sickness, disability, and premature death was taken essentially at its own evaluation.

I have no difficulty in dating the origin of my own doubts about the conventional assessment of the work of doctors. They began when I went to a London hospital as a medical student after several years of graduate research in the Departments of Biochemistry

ix

at McGill and Human Anatomy at Oxford. There were two
things that struck me, almost at once. One was the absence of
any real interest among clinical teachers in the origin of disease,
apart from its pathological and clinical manifestations; the other
was that whether the prescribed treatment was of any value to the
patient was often hardly noticed, particularly in internal medicine.
(On the latter point, although not the former, the approach in
surgery and obstetrics was somewhat different.) I adopted the
practice of asking myself at the bedside whether we were making
anyone any wiser or any better, and soon came to the conclusion
that most of the time we were not. Indeed there seemed to be an
inverse relation between the interest of a disease to the doctor and
the usefulness of its treatment to the patient. Neurology, for
example, was highly regarded and attracted some of the best
minds because of the fascination of its diagnostic problems; but
for the patient with multiple sclerosis, Parkinson's disease, amyo-
trophic lateral sclerosis, and most other serious neurological conditions, the precision of the diagnosis which was the focus of
medical interest made not the slightest difference to the outcome.
If the gifted neurologists had private qualms about the usefulness
of their efforts they gave no indication of them, at least in the
presence of students. Venereology, in contrast, although it provided the valuable treatment of syphilis and contributed to prevention of the spread of gonorrhoea, was held in low esteem; so
too were some useful surgical procedures including, remarkably,
the surgery of accidents, perhaps the most successful of all therapeutic measures. Endocrinology, in which I had been working,
was in an intermediate position; through its researches it had
reached Burlington House,[1] although its practice was still not far
removed from that of the hygienic stores which dispensed re-
juvenants on the Charing Cross Road. I concluded that if I were
St Peter, admitting to Heaven on the basis of achievement on
earth, I would accept on proof of identity the accident surgeons,
the dentists and, with a few doubts, the obstetricians; all, it should
be noted in passing, dealing mainly with healthy people. The rest
I would refer to some celestial equivalent of Ellis Island, for close
and prolonged inspection of their credentials.

1. At that time the home of the Royal Society.

Preface

The opportunity and incentive to consider more deeply what was initially little more than an undocumented impression, came through my appointment to the Chair of Social Medicine at Birmingham. In the early 1940s some senior teachers had come to the conclusion that a medical school located in the industrial Midlands should have a department of occupational health, and an application was made to the Nuffield Provincial Hospitals Trust which was known to be interested in the subject and had made a grant for the same purpose to Manchester. The Trust offered to finance a chair of social medicine but not of occupational health; so on the sound principle of not looking a gift horse in the mouth the University accepted the grant and changed its intentions. However one of the attractions of the term social medicine at that time was that each could interpret it in his own way, and I doubt whether the change of title was considered important.

My own association with the new department was fortuitous, to say the least. I had been interested in another post (in the Department of Medicine), when the University, having advertised the Chair twice with disappointing results and presumably at a loss about what to do next, invited me to submit an application. The only requirement, apparently, was that I should be seen and not objected to by Sir Farquhar Buzzard, then Regius Professor of Medicine at Oxford and advisor to the Nuffield interest. I met Sir Farquhar in his rooms at Christ Church at lunchtime; but not for lunch, as I could not fail to perceive from the fact that the College servant was preparing the table for one. For a moment I thought I might find myself in the position of the courtiers of Louis XIV, who attended patiently while their monarch supped singly and in silence. However the interview was short and scarcely delayed his meal, to which no doubt I largely owe the fact that he evidently raised no objection to my appointment. The background was illuminated further when I eventually took possession of a room in the Medical School, shared previously by the part-time teacher of public health (Dr G. A. Auden, father of the poet) and the lecturer in forensic medicine, and filled with drains, waterpipes, contraceptives, and numerous other objects of forensic and nine-teenth-century public health interest. The room also contained the applications for the post to which I had just been appointed.

After perusing them I could see the University's difficulty. One candidate included among his credentials that having committed himself to no line of activity he was free to develop in any; another stated that he had been advised by his doctor to seek lighter work; a third had the misfortune to name a referee who wrote that the applicant did not suffer fools gladly, always an unwise thing to say to a selection committee, since it makes them uncomfortable.

In the Department of Social Medicine the contribution of medicine to improvement in health was a subject of intermittent interest but no detailed research until 1953 when H. J. Habakkuk published an article on the growth of population in England during the eighteenth century. In it he questioned the traditional interpretation, proposed by Talbot Griffith in 1926 and accepted by most social historians, that the increase was due to a decline of the death-rate brought about by advances in medicine. Habakkuk considered that the medical measures of that period looked insufficient to account for the rise of population and turned to the possibility, attractive to some historians, that it resulted from an increase of the birth-rate which was secondary to economic and industrial developments. Our own view (I speak here also for my colleagues subsequently associated with this work) was that Habakkuk's estimate of medical measures was correct, but that nevertheless a fall of mortality was a more plausible explanation for the growth of population than a rise of fertility. A first paper on this subject (in 1955) was followed by others concerned with population growth in the nineteenth and twentieth centuries, and in a recent book (*The Modern Rise of Population*[1]) I have attempted a comprehensive interpretation of the increase of population from the eighteenth century to the present day. This book was first suggested to me by an Oxford historian, John Cooper, but I did not think seriously of tackling it until 1973, when at a meeting in Pavia I discovered that there was a considerable industry among French and Italian historians working on such unrewarding topics as the decline of plague and inoculation against smallpox in the eighteenth century.

1. Edward Arnold, London, 1976.

In the meantime I had come to see that recognition of the limited impact of medical procedures was a key which would unlock many doors. My own interest in it was initially, and is still primarily, in its significance to medicine and health services, and this is the theme of the present monograph. To state it simply: misinterpretation of the major influences, particularly personal medical care, on past and future improvements in health has led to misuse of resources and distortion of the role of medicine.

Since this statement may appear to have an affinity with the conclusions reached by Professor Cochrane in his notable Rock Carling Lecture on *Effectiveness and Efficiency,* I must try to distinguish between our approaches. I think of him as an itinerant preacher who emerges at intervals from his Welsh retreat to admonish the faithful for their failure to submit all aspects of their lives and works to scientific appraisal by randomized controlled trials; myself I see as an academic Billy Graham who bears the glad tidings of health for the taking to a grateful people. The distinction will be worth a closer examination.

In *Effectiveness and Efficiency* Cochrane criticized the organization of medical services and to a lesser extent, or at least more briefly, the direction of medical research. The grounds for his criticism of services were two-fold: many medical procedures and services have not been tested for their effectiveness and a considerable number of those which have been assessed were found to be unsatisfactory; and there are gross inequalities in standards of services, particularly between the 'care' and 'cure' sectors. Although few people are likely to question the last assertion, it should be noted that it was not based on, and probably does not permit or require, the same kind of validation as a clinical procedure. Finally, although the monograph refers briefly to environmental and behavioural influences (the importance of population policy was emphasized in the Conclusions), it was concerned mainly with clinical procedures and services.

What should be observed about this approach is that it does not suggest that there is anything seriously wrong with the traditional lines of health services and medical research, apart from the imbalance in investment between care and cure. Moreover the last is a pragmatic rather than a conceptual criticism. What is said to be lacking is scientific evaluation of measures before they are introduced, and it is implied that if everything were submitted to randomized controlled trials, effective clinical procedures and services would in time appear (an endorsement of Proust's view that from the mass of errors there would emerge many truths).

It need hardly be said that Cochrane's emphasis on the need for critical appraisal of medical measures was entirely justified, and being based largely on his own extensive experience had an impact which no other approach could have matched. Indeed as noted on the first page of this Preface, our health traditions have had no difficulty in living with criticism from outside; but they are more vulnerable to attack from within, to the suggestion—not that medical activities are misdirected (an unlikely conclusion from a son of University College Hospital who has laboured in the vineyards of the MRC), but that they are not sufficiently scientific. However I see the exchange as an opening round in a long engagement, in which the premises on which health, and particularly medical activities are based, require to be explored. My own position, in distinction from that of Professor Cochrane, is, briefly, as follows.

Medical science and services are misdirected, and society's investment in health is not well used, because they rest on an erroneous assumption about the basis of human health. It is assumed that the body can be regarded as a machine whose protection from disease and its effects depends primarily on internal intervention. The approach has led to indifference to the external influences and personal behaviour which are the predominant determinants of health. It has also resulted in the relative neglect of the majority of sick people who provide no scope for the internal measures which are at the centre of medical interest.

This book presents the grounds for these assertions, and examines their significance to health services and to medical education and research.

I should not like to end this Preface without expressing my indebtedness to my colleague, Professor R. G. Record. We have worked together for thirty years, and I have discussed with him nearly every point related to medical achievement and population growth. If I have been able to avoid serious errors in this wide and treacherous subject, it has been due largely to his sound advice, particularly on clinical matters.

It is also a pleasure for me to thank Mrs Eileen Armstrong and my secretary, Mrs Wendy Greenaway, for the care they have taken with the preparation of the typescript.

I

Introduction
Concepts of health and disease

The aims of this book are: (a) to examine the validity of a concept which is rarely stated explicitly but on which medical activities largely rest, namely that human health depends essentially on a mechanistic approach based on understanding of the structure and function of the body and of the disease processes that affect it; and (b) to consider the significance of the conclusions for medicine, particularly in relation to health services, medical education, and medical research. These themes are discussed in the two sections into which the book is divided, the first concerned with the determinants of health and the second with the role of medicine.

Although the mechanistic approach is predominant it is not the only one which has been taken to improve man's health. In his splendid account of the evolution of health concepts Dubos referred to the dual nature of medicine which resulted from ideas which have been promoted with varying emphasis in all periods down to the present day: health preserved by way of life and health restored by treatment of disease. Both were to be found in the classical tradition:

The myths of Hygieia and Asclepius symbolise the never-ending oscillation between two different points of view in medicine. For the worshippers of Hygieia, health is the natural order of things, a positive attribute to which men are entitled if they govern their lives wisely. According to them, the most important function of medicine is to discover and teach the natural laws which will ensure a man a healthy mind in a healthy body. More sceptical, or wiser in the ways of the world, the followers of Asclepius believe that the chief role of the physician is to treat disease, to restore health by correcting any imperfections caused by the accidents of birth or life.[1]

The preservative approach was certainly in the minds of the social and medical reformers of the eighteenth and nineteenth centuries,

1. Dubos, R., *Mirage of Health* (London: George Allen and Unwin Ltd, 1960), p. 109.

I

and it is to be found in the public health activities which resulted from their efforts and have continued and developed to the present day.

Philosophically the seventeenth century was a turning point in the balance between the two concepts. Galileo had shown that scientific methods were capable of providing a mechanical interpretation of the physical world, and Descartes saw no reason why the same principles should not be extended to living things. He conceived of the body as a machine, governed entirely by the laws of physics, which might be taken apart and reassembled if its structure and function were fully understood. His theories seemed to find confirmation in the first major development in modern physiology, Kepler's description of the dioptric mechanism by which the eye produces the retinal image. This advance resulted from the application of technical knowledge available in second-century Alexandria, but which no Greek would have thought of bringing to the study of the living body. A little later there was an even more dramatic demonstration of the validity of the mechanistic approach in Harvey's discovery of the circulation of the blood, which Descartes, needless to say, warmly welcomed.

In the present context there are three aspects of the hypothesis to be considered: the relation between mind and body; the body interpreted as a machine; and the body controlled as a machine.

The first subject need not detain us, although it has been the focus of endless controversy at the interface between science and theology. Briefly, while Descartes as a scientist could accept a physical explanation for the body, as a religious man he was unable to accept it for the mind; so he found it necessary to distinguish between mind and body, and he introduced what Ryle described as the Category-mistake, the notion of the mind as a ghost in the body as a machine.[1] Temporarily at least, this explanation furnished a reconciliation of sorts between the results of the new science and the traditional doctrines of the soul. However, although this problem has engaged the attention of philosophers and theologians for centuries, for many scientists educated since the First World War I suspect it has scarcely existed. Unencum-

1. Ryle, G., *The Concept of Mind* (London: Hutchinson's University Library, 1950).

2

bered by preconceptions derived from religion or scholastic philosophy, they have never thought of the mind as something which exists apart from the physical structure of the body. Their problems arise mainly from the other implications of the Cartesian hypothesis: the body conceived as a machine and the body controlled as a machine.

There is no difficulty today in accepting that the body can be understood as a machine, of which knowledge has advanced continuously from the seventeenth century; slowly at first, but very rapidly at the cellular level since the nineteenth century and at a molecular level in the twentieth. In parallel with the understanding of structure and function there was an increase in knowledge of disease processes, including, in the case of infectious diseases, recognition of disease agents. It is hardly surprising that the transformation of human health which occurred in the same period was attributed to the new knowledge, that the improvement in the performance of the body as a machine was assumed to be due to its control as a machine.

However this is an assumption which must be examined carefully. In the first place it should be noted that in the past three centuries conditions of life have improved more than in any previous period in man's history. For large populations the chronic problem of malnutrition has been solved; some of the most serious threats, particularly those associated with water and food, have been removed from the environment; and for the first time on an extensive scale human populations have limited their reproduction to a level consistent with basic resources. In assessing the contribution of medical measures based on understanding of the structure and function of the body, it is clearly essential to consider the extent to which the advance in health was due, not to intervention in the working of the machine, but to improvement in the conditions under which it operates.

There is another reason for caution before endorsing the conventional explanation for the advance in man's health: the fact that quite a different interpretation must be accepted for the improvement in health of other living things. The brief discussion which follows will be concerned with animals, although many of the conclusions would be equally true for plants.

3

The key to the riddle presented by the health of living things is the relation of fertility to mortality. Both have evolved through natural selection; but they have not evolved in balance, in the sense that numbers born are restricted with regard for the resources of the environment and the numbers that can survive. A contrary view, that animals limit their reproduction by social and biological restraints,[1] was strongly challenged,[2] and since it has no relevance to human experience in the past few centuries it will not be considered here.

The alternative, and I believe more convincing interpretation, suggests that the size of natural populations is controlled by density-dependent mortality. In wild birds and some other animals (Lack mentioned carnivorous mammals, certain rodents, large fish where not fished, and a few insects) the level of mortality is determined mainly by the availability of food. However there are other animals, possibly many more, in which, although numbers are limited ultimately by food supplies, these limits are not usually reached because population size is restricted by predators, including insect parasites, and disease.[2]

On this interpretation the essential requirements for reduction of mortality and improvement in health of animal populations are (*a*) equating of food supplies and population size, by increasing the amount of food and limiting numbers, and (*b*) removal of other causes of mortality, particularly predators, including in some cases human predators, and parasites.

This theoretically derived programme is in accord with what has actually happened in domestication of plants and animals. Their numbers and distribution are controlled; more and better food is provided: manure and fertilizers for plants, foodstuffs in a variety of forms for animals; and domesticated plants and animals are protected so far as possible from environmental hazards.

Another method of outstanding importance is selective breeding, which has been used with all domesticated animals except the elephant. (Elephants rarely breed in captivity.) This approach has been employed to accentuate characters desired by man, some-

1. Wynne-Edwards, V. C., *Animal Dispersion in Relation to Social Behaviour* (Edinburgh: Oliver and Boyd, 1972).
2. Lack, D., *Population Studies of Birds* (Oxford: Clarendon Press, 1966).

4

times with side-effects on health from production of pure strains which are less resistant to micro-organisms. But cross-breeding has been used to produce hardier stocks by heterosis.

The methods which have been exploited in plant and animal husbandry are essentially population methods which owe little to understanding of structure and function. It is fairly obvious why this approach has been preferred to physical or chemical manipulation of individual plants or animals. In the first place, except in the case of pets and unique specimens such as race-horses and prize cattle, man has little interest in individual examples of species other than his own. Secondly, it is more economical to deal with large numbers in preference to identifying and controlling single specimens. And finally, a conclusion which is particularly important for human health, population methods are far more effective than individual methods. Indeed when they are fully applied there is little need for direct intervention, for under favourable conditions the large majority of those born alive remain healthy.

To what extent is it possible to extrapolate from other animals to man? Until the eighteenth century the human situation was analogous, if not homologous, to that of animals in their natural habitats; numbers born were greatly in excess of numbers that could survive, and population size was limited by density-dependent mortality. There is no evidence of effective restriction of population growth, either by deliberate control of reproduction or by instinctive restraints of the kind suggested by Wynne-Edwards in other animals.[1] The high level of mortality was due to starvation, disease, and homicide in its multiple forms.

In these circumstances human health provided scope for the methods which led to improvement in the health of domesticated animals. Like other living things, man has been exposed to rigorous natural selection, and the large majority of those born alive are healthy in the sense that they are adapted to the environment in which they live. The primary need is for sufficient food, which requires both an increase in food supplies and limitation of numbers. Man also needs protection from certain hazards in the physical environment, particularly those which lead to exposure to infective organisms. The notable difference between human

1. Wynne-Edwards, V. C., *Animal Dispersion in Relation to Social Behaviour.*

and other animal experience in relation to health results from ethical restraints which prohibit public control of reproduction. But man is uniquely educable, and can learn voluntarily to limit family size. In this way a self-imposed behavioural change may achieve the same result as the restrictions applied to other animals.

However the approach to biology and medicine established in the seventeenth century was an engineering one based on a physical model; its consequences are even more conspicuous today, largely because the resources of the physical and chemical sciences are so much greater. Physics, chemistry, and biology are considered to be the sciences basic to medicine; medical education begins with study of the structure and function of the body, continues with examination of disease processes and ends with clinical instruction on selected sick people. Medical service is dominated by the image of the acute hospital where the technological resources are concentrated, and much less attention is given to environmental and behavioural determinants of disease, or to the needs of sick people who are not thought to provide scope for investigation or therapy. Medical science also reflects the mechanistic concept, for example in the attention given to the chemical basis of inheritance and the immunological response to transplanted organs. These researches are strictly in accord with the physical model, the first being thought to lead to control of gene structure and the second to replacement of diseased organs by normal ones. The question therefore, is not whether the engineering approach is predominant in medicine, which would hardly be disputed, but whether it is seriously deficient as a conceptualization of the problems of human health.

The first part of this book is concerned with an examination of this issue. There are at least three approaches which might be taken to assessment of the determinants of human health. One possibility would be to examine, where possible by controlled trials, the effectiveness and efficiency of medical procedures and services, as well as of other influences, such as food and hygienic measures, which contribute powerfully to health. This approach has been employed with great advantage in a limited number of cases; but it presents formidable technical, ethical, and administrative difficulties and it is hardly conceivable that within the

6

foreseeable future it could provide a comprehensive appraisal of all the major determinants of health. I have therefore restricted attention to the other possibilities.

Chapter 2 outlines a conceptual approach. It suggests that if we are thinking of disease origins rather than disease mechanisms, the most fundamental division is between abnormalities determined irreversibly at fertilization and those which are manifested only in an appropriate environment. Among the latter there is an important practical distinction between congenital conditions in which the environmental influences are prenatal and those, including most common disease, in which they are probably post-natal. Although post-natal influences vary greatly in type, it is suggested that it is upon their identification and control that hopes for the solution of the problems of the common diseases largely rest. This approach can often succeed in spite of deficient knowledge of disease mechanisms.

The next three chapters present the third approach, an examination of historical evidence; they are based on data for England and Wales which are perhaps the most satisfactory for this purpose. It is shown that the decline of mortality, the main evidence of improvement in health, was due essentially to a reduction of deaths from infectious diseases. (The only non-infective causes which appear to have decreased substantially before the twentieth century were infanticide and starvation.) Chapter 4 investigates the reasons for the decline of the infections, and Chapter 5 considers non-infective conditions which were associated with about a quarter of the reduction of mortality since 1900.

The conclusions concerning the determinants of man's health are brought together in Chapter 6. The predominant influences which led to the improvement in health in the past three centuries were nutritional, environmental (particularly control of water and food), and behavioural; the last through the change in reproductive practices which limited population growth. The major influences are reconsidered in the light of the change in health problems which followed the decline of the infections, and it is concluded that in advanced countries health is still determined mainly by personal behaviour and the environment. However there is this difference, that the influences which result from the

7

individual's behaviour (smoking, diet, exercise, etc.) are now relatively more important than those which depend on action by society. The contribution of personal medical measures remains tertiary in relation to the predominant behavioural and environmental influences.

Part Two discusses the implications of these conclusions for medicine. In relation to health services (Chapter 7) there are two important issues. The first concerns the extent of medical involvement in the behavioural and environmental determinants of health. Many people would say that such matters can safely be left in the hands of other health workers, a view that has attractions for some doctors who would be glad to be rid of responsibility, particularly for non-personal services. However it is argued that a contribution is needed from medical specialists in environmental medicine and from all practising doctors in relation to patients' behaviour which prejudices their health.

The second important issue is the significance of the conclusion that personal medical care does not make a large contribution to health. The design of health services is based on quite a different assumption: that investigation and treatment of disease are critical not only to recovery from acute illness, but also to long-term health prospects. It is this belief which is thought to justify the large investment in acute services, and to excuse the relative neglect of other patients, the majority, among the mentally ill, the aged sick, and the mentally subnormal. In the light of the reappraisal of influences on health what is needed is not merely a transfer of resources from acute to other services, but a rethinking of the whole relationship between the various phases of care. It will also be necessary to have a more critical approach to the quality of care, including under this term: standards (how well we do what we do); effectiveness (whether what we do is worth doing); and efficiency (whether what we do makes better use of health resources than the available alternatives). Finally Chapter 7 has something to say about the relation of doctors to other health workers, already a vexed question in some fields and one which is likely to arise in others.

The implications of the conclusions from Part One for medical education are considered in Chapter 8. A health service can be no

8

more enlightened than the minds of those who provide it, and if medical responsibilities are to be enlarged it is essential to have appropriate changes in the education of the doctor. A greater emphasis is needed on the origins of disease, the effectiveness and risks of treatment, and the care of patients who have completed investigation and treatment or who are of a kind not often seen in teaching hospitals. However, the main influence on students is undoubtedly the range of service and research interests exhibited at the teaching centre.

The direction of biomedical research has been determined by the belief that improvement in health depends essentially on knowledge of the body and its diseases, applied mainly through personal medical intervention in the form of immunization and therapy. In Chapter 9 it is shown that this interpretation is not in accord with past experience: the modern improvement in health was initiated and carried quite a long way with little assistance from science and technology, and until the twentieth century the contribution of science was essentially of a non-personal kind, particularly in relation to agriculture and control of water and food. When considered in relation to the concepts outlined in Chapter 2, these findings suggest that in medical research the main emphasis should be on disease origins rather than disease mechanisms, although there is need for continued attention to both. In the light of these conclusions suggestions are made about an alternative, or perhaps more accurately, about a modified approach to research problems.

The final chapter brings together a few general reflections on the role of medicine. It examines some sharply contrasted ideas which are much discussed at the present time: that residual health problems will be solved by extension of the traditional research and service approach, and the amendment: that the dream of advance through knowledge acquired in the laboratory and applied at the bedside has faded, and little more can be expected from biomedical research; that the goal of improved health is largely illusory, since with changing conditions of life, health problems must be expected to change but not to disappear; and that the role of medicine is essentially sinister: for many reasons, but particularly because it usurps the right of the individual to face, deal with, and bear his own health problems. Finally an attempt is made to outline the medical role in terms which take account of the nature of the residual health problems, and of the contribution which medicine can be expected to make to their solution in the future.

Part One

Determinants of health

2

Inheritance, environment, and disease

When I began medical training at a London teaching hospital just before the Second World War, some observant clinicians were already aware that cancer of the lung was becoming a common disease. The surgeon who specialized in thoracic work referred frequently to the seriousness of the problem, and urged that 'Doctors must become cancer of the lung conscious, in the same way that they are already cancer of the bowel conscious.' We were told that the condition was being discovered too late for surgery to be effective, and the solution, it was implied, was in early diagnosis. So far as I can recall, there was little discussion of aetiology or of the possibility that the disease might be due to influences which could be modified or removed.

This approach to the most remarkable epidemic of the twentieth century was characteristic of the approach to disease in general. There was usually a brief comment on aetiology. (We were taught that there were five theories of toxaemia of pregnancy: if the student mentioned only four, that was one too few, and if six, one too many.) However, the discussion was mainly in mechanistic terms; in hypertension, for example, it was concerned with experimental evidence that restriction of the blood supply to the kidney raises pressure, rather than with the distribution of arterial pressure in the general population or the reasons why natural selection has failed to eliminate a serious and common disease. The focus of interest was on pathology, diagnosis, and treatment, and in the case of treatment, on what was done rather than whether it was worth doing. If clinical teachers had been asked why patients have diseases such as diabetes, hypertension, and rheumatoid arthritis, most would have discussed insulin, renal function, and allergy. And if pressed to go further and say why the underlying abnormalities exist, they would probably have referred rather vaguely to constitution, by which they would have meant inherited constitution. Infectious diseases, it would have been agreed, were essentially of environmental origin; but others, including particularly the common diseases of middle and late life, were considered to be inborn. The patient had diabetes because he had a defective pancreas and, if the matter were taken further, which usually it was not, the pancreatic abnormality was attributable to his genes.

Today the discussion of aetiology is somewhat extended, and many teachers give due attention to the importance of smoking, exercise, and diet. Moreover these influences are no longer considered only in the academic terms of a generation earlier; by their teaching and example some conscientious clinicians try to modify the practice of their students and the behaviour of their patients. Nevertheless in medicine as a whole the traditional mechanistic approach remains essentially unchanged; and it will remain unchanged so long as the concept of disease is based on a physico-chemical model.

CLASSIFICATION OF DISEASE

Textbooks of medicine rarely include a full discussion of the origin and nature of disease processes. One well-known text[1] has sections on 'genetic principles', and 'environmental factors in disease'; but these themes are considered separately, and the section on the environment is concerned mainly with topics such as heat and cold, pollution and poisoning, rather than with the relation between heredity and environment in the causation of disease.

This subject is discussed in the genetic section which is included in some, but by no means all, textbooks of medicine. Geneticists have of course written perceptively about the basis of disease, and some have examined the feasibility of control in the light of the conclusions (for example, whether familial concentration of a disease implies that it is unlikely to be influenced by environmental measures). In general, however, and understandably, they have approached the subject against the background of genetic

1. Cecil, R. F., and Loeb, R. F., in Beeson, P. B., and McDermott, W. (eds), *Textbook of Medicine* (Philadelphia, London, Toronto: W. B. Saunders Company, 1971), pp. 4, 24.

interest, and diseases are usually divided into three classes: uncommon conditions associated with single genes; conditions (common at conception and uncommon at birth) associated with chromosomal aberrations; and common diseases whose genetic basis is obscure.

However if the approach to aetiology is an operational one whose aim is prevention or some other means of control, an alternative distinction can be made between diseases according to whether they are or are not determined at fertilization. For serious conditions determined irreversibly at fertilization, the only complete solutions would be avoidance of conception or elimination during pregnancy by abortion. In contrast, diseases not established at fertilization could in principle be prevented if it were possible to identify and modify adverse environmental influences.

DISEASES DETERMINED AT FERTILIZATION

There are three types of diseases in this class, distinguishable according to whether the genetic abnormality can be seen, predicted, or inferred.

Chromosomal aberrations. Chromosomal aberrations can be seen under the microscope, and current estimates suggest that at the beginning of pregnancy they are present in about 5 per cent of embryos. Having regard to the complexity of events at fertilization, it is perhaps surprising that they are not more common. The large majority are eliminated by abortion (more than a third of spontaneous abortions appear to have abnormal chromosomes), so that their incidence in live-births is low.

Single-gene disorders. These are the simply inherited abnormalities, dominant, recessive, or X-linked, whose distribution can be predicted on Mendelian principles. Where the fertility of those affected is low or absent, the frequency of the genes is reduced by natural selection, and the continued appearance of conditions such as haemophilia is attributed to new mutations. Phenylketonuria and a few similar conditions can now be treated with some success, and in time, no doubt, it will be possible to treat effectively some other single gene disorders. In this case the effects of the abnormalities would no longer be determined irreversibly at fertilization, and in an operational classification they could be transferred to conditions which can be prevented or corrected by environmental measures (which in this context include treatment).

Other abnormalities determined at fertilization. Genetic disorders which are simply inherited or due to chromosomal aberrations are observed in about 0·5 per cent of births; in classifications of disease the rest, the large majority, are usually considered together as common diseases which are polygenic. Although this classification is accurate, it brings under the common diseases some which are determined at fertilization. They are not associated with detectable abnormalities of single genes or chromosomes, and their inevitability from the time of fertilization can only be inferred. I refer particularly to certain diseases and disabilities of late life.

This interpretation rests on a conclusion which would hardly be disputed, that the maximum duration of life of a species is genetically determined. Of course it may be shortened by environmental accidents of many kinds; but it cannot be prolonged significantly beyond the normal span. Examples of exceptionally long lives of more than a hundred years are sometimes cited as evidence that life-expectancy could be increased by internal or external measures; they prove only that like other characters such as stature and intelligence, the 'natural' duration of life is distributed over a wide range. With such characters the range could be modified by selective breeding; but only if society were prepared to accept a single major objective and to introduce stringent control of reproduction in order to achieve it. Neither possibility seems desirable or likely.

If the maximum duration of life is determined at the time of fertilization, so too, it seems reasonable to believe, are some of the diseases and disabilities associated with its end. There are mystics and others who appear to find suffering rewarding; but if allowed to choose, most people would probably elect to die in late life during sleep from a myocardial infarction or cerebral haemorrhage: the Almighty's approximation to the clinical efficiency of the abattoir. Unfortunately the execution is frequently bungled, so that the programmed end is preceded by a period of ill-health, caused by the breakdown of non-essential organs, such as eyes, ears, or joints, or by the partial collapse of an essential one, such as the brain, the heart, or the kidney, usually from a vascular accident or deficiency.

However, it is safer to conclude that some disorders of late life are genetic than to specify the ones that are. It is not long since most of the ill-named degenerative diseases would have been labelled *en bloc* as inborn, or constitutional; indeed, in his inaugural address at University College ('An Unsolved Problem of Biology') Medawar[1] examined the possibility that many serious conditions are genetically determined and occur in late life because they are unaffected or less affected by natural selection. However, it is now clear that cancer of the lung, chronic bronchitis, and some forms of heart disease are largely determined by the environment, and it is probable that the same is true for many other diseases, including most cancers. Nevertheless it would be unreasonably optimistic to believe that all the disorders of the elderly are of this kind, and it is quite likely that some defects of brain, vision, hearing, and loco-motion (for example) are the result of a differential rate of wearing-out of organs which is determined by genes.

The grouping of this third class of conditions with the previous two, for which there is a good deal of knowledge of the genetic basis, may seem unsatisfactory; and so it is, if we are concerned primarily with the underlying mechanisms. But if our interest is in disease control, the most useful distinction is between conditions which could be prevented only by contraception or abortion, and those in which there is the possibility of prevention by environ-mental measures. It is on these grounds that some abnormalities, particularly in late life, deserve to be included among diseases determined at fertilization.

DISEASES NOT DETERMINED AT FERTILIZATION

The large majority of diseases and disabilities are neither simply inherited nor otherwise determined irreversibly at fertilization; they are usually described as multifactorial, by which is meant that they are caused by interaction between multiple environ-mental and genetic influences. All common diseases that have been

1. Medawar, P. B., The Uniqueness of the Individual (London: Methuen & Co. Ltd, 1957), p. 44.

17

studied are to some extent familial, and attempts have been made to attribute them to a few specific genes, or to a single gene of low penetrance whose effects are irregularly manifested. The results are not convincing, and take us little beyond the conclusion that their genetic basis is obscure.

The questions of most practical importance in relation to these diseases are: Is it possible to assess the relative importance of heredity and environment? and Would such an assessment enable us to judge the feasibility of preventing a disease by modifying the environment?

NATURE AND NURTURE

The difficulty of assessing, and particularly of assessing numerically, the respective contributions of heredity and environment was discussed at some length by Hogben in *Nature and Nurture*.[1] He examined the results of temperature changes in two mutations of *Drosophila* which differ in the number of eye facets: the number of facets varies with the temperature of the environment in which the larvae develop. It was observed that there was a difference between the number of facets (*a*) in the two stocks at the same temperature attributable to the genetic difference and (*b*) in the same stock at different temperatures, attributable to the environmental difference. But it was not possible to assess the contribution of heredity and environment when comparing the number of facets in the two stocks in different environments. Hogben concluded: 'We are on safe ground when we speak of genetic difference between two groups measured in one and the same environment or in speaking of a difference due to the environment when identical stocks are measured under different conditions of development.' But we are not on equally safe ground when we speak of the contribution of heredity and environment to the measurements of genetically different individuals measured in different kinds of environment.

The reader who is unfamiliar with this reasoning and finds it difficult to follow the results of the experiment on *Drosophila*

1. Hogben, L., *Nature and Nurture*, William Withering Memorial Lecture, 1935 (London: George Allen and Unwin Ltd, 1945), p. 96.

without visual illustration, would be rewarded by reading the discussion in Hogben's classic monograph written more than forty years ago. However, the essence of the argument may be clarified by reference to a human disease. Let us consider two individuals who differ in their genetically determined proneness to diabetes. In rural Africa, on the traditional diet, neither would exhibit the disease; in a western country, on refined foods with a high intake of sugar, the more prone might be affected and the other might not. We can conclude that the difference in the experience of the more prone in the two countries was due to the change in diet; and that the difference in the disease experience of the two individuals in the western country was probably attributable to their genes. But comparing the experience of the two in different environments, we can arrive at no meaningful conclusion about the contributions of nature and nurture.

In the light of these difficulties we need to be extremely cautious when attempting to assess, particularly in quantitative terms, the influence of heredity and environment in the causation of human disease. There are no pure strains and there are few constant environments; conclusions must therefore be based on investigations which are no more than approximations to the experimental models.

The only individuals with identical genes are monozygotic twins, and observed differences in their disease experience can usually be attributed to their environments, prenatal or post-natal. (Even about this conclusion there must be a reservation: Edwards has noted that 'differences between similar cells in similar tissues must be largely fortuitous and it would be wrong to infer that, because identical twins show little similarity in their liability to some diseases, particularly such focal diseases as neoplasia, environmental features must, therefore, be important'.)[1] However, the matter is usually considered the other way round: if identical twins are consistently both affected in different environments, the abnormality is said to be determined by their common genes. The usual procedure is to identify pairs in which at least one twin is affected, and inquire how frequently the other twin has the same

1. Edwards, J. H., 'The genetic basis of common disease', *American Journal of Medicine*, 34 (1963), p. 631.

condition (ie, is concordant). The results are then compared with those of dizygotic twins and, sometimes, other relatives. In no common disease is concordance 100 per cent; but when it is consistently high in twins exposed to different environments, say over 80 per cent and at least twice the rate in non-identical twins, it seems permissible to conclude that the condition is largely determined by genes of high specificity. In practice it is of course difficult to find a considerable number of identical twins with a disorder, even a common one, who have been observed in different environments. It must also be remembered that twins are unusual in both their intra-uterine environment and their up-bringing, so there must be reservations when generalizing from experience of twins to that of single births.

The second model examines the disease experience of individuals who differ genetically but share the same environment. The usual method is to compare identical twins whose genes are common, with other relatives (parents, children, sibs) in whom half the genes are the same. Different genotypes are also identifiable by blood groups and, less reliably, by markers such as race and colour. The general problem with this approach is uncertainty that the environments to which those compared have been exposed were the same, at least in respect of the features, often unknown, which are critical for the disease in question. Since close relatives share a common environment as well as common genes, it is hardly surprising that many diseases tend to run in families and from this observation alone no conclusion can be drawn about the contributions of heredity and environment.

The problem in applying the two models to the study of human disease is not therefore that they are wrong in principle, but that in practice it is often impossible to assemble the requisite data. It is difficult to find a large number of affected individuals of the same genotype (identical twins) exposed to a range of different environments, or of different genotypes exposed to the same environment. What is usually available is a comparison between different genotypes observed in different environments, and the interpretation is open to the objections referred to above.

In spite of these difficulties it is possible to arrive at tentative conclusions about the contribution of heredity and environment in some diseases. For example, nearly everyone who eats food infected by salmonella organisms suffers from gastro-enteritis, but only a small proportion of those exposed to respiratory tuberculosis contract the clinical disease. (On the latter point perhaps the best evidence is the low frequency of tuberculosis in wives of men who are sputum positive.) In the one case the salmonella organisms are a necessary and sufficient condition for the appearance of the disease in man; in the other the tubercle bacillus is a necessary but not a sufficient condition, since it requires the complement of the appropriate genotype. But does this distinction have much bearing on the feasibility of control?

FEASIBILITY OF CONTROL

This brings us to the second question concerning the common diseases: Does assessment of the contribution of nature and nurture enable us to judge the possibility of preventing a disease by modifying the environment? Since an appropriate environment is essential for the appearance of the common diseases, the important consideration is not the balance between nature and nurture, which in any case varies with the environment, but the practicability of identifying and removing the adverse influences.

In the case of infectious diseases this turns largely on the ways they are spread. It is relatively easy to interrupt transmission of water-borne diseases (such as cholera and typhoid) by control of the public supply; it is more difficult to prevent the spread of food-borne diseases (such as salmonella and staphylococcal poisoning) which requires strict personal hygiene; and it is often impossible to control airborne infections (such as pneumonia, influenza, and the common cold).

With non-communicable diseases the problems are much greater, and for a number of reasons. (*a*) The nature of the adverse influences may be unknown, as in schizophrenia and breast cancer. (*b*) The influences may be multiple, and hence difficult to assess, as in coronary artery disease. (*c*) Removal of the influences may require modification of behaviour which many people are reluctant to accept, as in cancer of the lung and road accidents. (*d*) But by far the most important restriction exists where the influences are prenatal, and difficult or impossible to recognize or control. Indeed, in relation to the feasibility of prevention, the distinction between congenital conditions and those determined after birth is more important than that between infections and non-communicable diseases; it is also more significant than the balance sheet of heredity and environment.

Against this background it can be seen that while infections and other common diseases differ in the ease of their control, they do not differ in the concept of their origin. In both cases, a certain genotype is needed; but it is manifested only in a suitable environment.

TABLE 2.1. *Estimates of prenatal deaths in 1838–54 and 1970: England and Wales.*

	Deaths per 1,000 conceptions	
	1838–54	1970
Spontaneous abortions	140	140
Legal abortions	Nil	70
Illegal abortions	50	10
Stillbirths	40	10
Total	230	230

This appraisal of heredity and environment in the aetiology of disease suggests that improvement in health is likely to result from elimination of environmental hazards, and to be in respect of conditions determined post-natally rather than prenatally. This conclusion is consistent with the age-trend of mortality in England and Wales between 1838–54 and 1970. Figure 2.1 shows the number of deaths per 1,000 conceptions for five age periods: prenatal, 0–14, 15–44, 45–64, and 65 and over. Mortality after birth was estimated by applying to the numbers live-born (estimated as 770 per 1,000 conceptions in both 1838–54 and 1970) data provided in English life tables for the relevant years. The only uncertainties are about prenatal losses, which are based on the figures in Table 2.1.

Contemporary estimates of the proportions of conceptions aborted spontaneously appear to be reasonably reliable and are about 140 per 1,000; there is no reason to believe that this figure has changed greatly since the mid nineteenth century. The frequency of legal abortions has risen rapidly since the liberalization of the grounds for abortion in 1968 and the figure for 1970 (70 per 1,000) is based on the number of legal abortions reported for that year.

Estimates of illegal abortions are the least reliable, and even today their number is unknown. But since the change in the law the number of pregnancies terminated illegally is probably small, and it has been assumed to be 10 per 1,000. The figure for 1838–54 (50 per 1,000) can be no more than a guess. On the one hand it seems certain that it was higher than it is today; on the other hand the methods available for inducing abortion were restricted and unwanted children were sometimes eliminated by infanticide.

The estimate for stillbirths in 1970 is based on the stillbirth rate (number of stillbirths per 1,000 stillbirths and live-births) for that year. For 1838–54, when stillbirths were not recorded, the rate has been assumed to be 50; the earliest recorded rate was 40 in 1928. This gives an estimate of approximately 40 stillbirths per 1,000 conceptions when account is taken of abortions.

On these estimates, the proportion of conceptions which terminate prenatally is of the order of 20 to 25 per cent. So far as can be judged from the limited data, the proportion has not altered substantially since the mid nineteenth century. However, since the revision of the abortion law in 1968 there has been a rapid increase in the number of legal abortions and, almost certainly, a decrease in illegal ones.

The figure (2.1) shows the remarkable change in the distribution of deaths during the past century. The notable features are: (*a*) little change in prenatal deaths (in spite of the decline of the stillbirth rate, whose contribution to the total of prenatal losses is not large); (*b*) a reduction in the number of deaths in early and middle life, marked at ages 0–14 and 15–44 and small at 45–64; and (*c*) an increase in deaths at 65 and over. This increase is of course due mainly to the greater number of people surviving to late life.

These trends in the age distribution of mortality are in accord with the interpretation outlined above. Prenatal mortality remains high, not because the causes of death are determined mainly at fertilization (although some, particularly the chromosomal

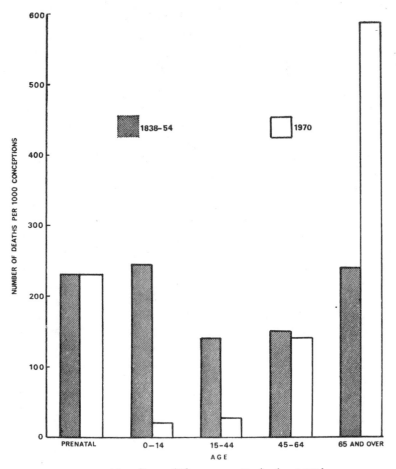

FIGURE 2.1. Mortality at different ages: England and Wales.

aberrations, undoubtedly are), but because the hazards associated with implantation and early embryonic development are largely unidentified. The great reduction of deaths in early life was due to environmental measures which reduced the prevalence and case-fatality of the predominant infections. But has there also been a substantial reduction of mortality at later ages, which is masked in Fig. 2.1 by the increased numbers surviving to late life?

National estimates indicate that there has been some increase in life expectation, say at ages 45 and over, but it has been much smaller than at younger ages. This might be interpreted to mean that the so-called degenerative diseases have not declined significantly, and cannot be expected to decline because they are determined at the time of fertilization and, being in the post-reproductive age period, are removed from the effects of natural selection.

A few decades ago it would have been difficult to reject this conclusion. However it is now clear that some of the commonest causes of death in middle and late life are largely determined by the environment; for example, chronic bronchitis and coronary artery disease. But the most impressive grounds for believing that many deaths in this age period are preventable is the evidence that most cancers are due to influences which in principle could be modified.[1] I shall refer briefly to three of the common cancers: of the lung, intestine, and breast.

The evidence linking smoking and cancer of the lung is well known and need not be restated; however it is worth noting that it meets epidemiological requirements which might be regarded as analogous to Koch's postulates in respect of the infections.

1. There is an epidemic of the disease.

2. A plausible agent (smoking) is associated with the disease.

3. The use of the agent has increased and the increase is in the expected temporal relation to the epidemic of the disease (in both sexes).

4. Removal of the agent has lowered mortality from the disease (in doctors).

In respect of cancer of the intestine it has been suggested that the frequent occurrence in advanced countries of a condition which is rare in rural communities of developing countries may be due to the change in diet, particularly refinement of food and removal of fibre. If this explanation is correct it is understandable that two of the four lines of evidence listed above cannot be met. For the refinement of food began long before cause of death was registered; in *Eugenie Grandet,* written in the 1830s, Balzac referred to the separation of the bran from the flour at the mill of the old

1. Doll, R., *Prevention of Cancer. Pointers from Epidemiology.* Rock Carling Monograph (Nuffield Provincial Hospitals Trust, 1967), p. 129.

miser. There are therefore no records of the onset of the epidemic of the disease or of increased consumption of the possible causal agent (refined foods).

In the case of breast cancer, variation in frequency in different sections of the population, particularly in relation to fertility, provides strong evidence of environmental influence; but again, and for obvious reasons, the detailed evidence is deficient. In diseases affecting the respiratory and digestive tracts it seems reasonable to consider agents entering the nose and the mouth; in a disease (such as cancer of the breast) affecting the reproductive system, we think first of influences on reproduction. Large changes in reproductive practices, perhaps the most profound in human history, have been associated in the past century with the transition from high to low birth-rates. They have modified the age at first pregnancy, the interval between pregnancies, the age at last pregnancy and the total number of pregnancies, as well as associated practices such as intercourse, contraception, and breast-feeding. It seems quite possible that one or more of these changes has been associated with the increase in prevalence of breast cancer; but if so the trends were too early to be demonstrated in national records.

Considered as a whole, however, in spite of the deficiencies the evidence concerning most cancers and some other diseases of middle and late life suggests strongly that they are not exceptions to the general conclusion—that the common diseases are attributable to environmental influences, although they vary considerably in the feasibility of their control. This conclusion is not inconsistent with recognition that some disorders of the elderly are genetically determined, in the sense that, like the maximum duration of life, they are programmed at the time of fertilization.

CONCLUSIONS

I shall now attempt to summarize conclusions which follow from this appraisal of heredity and environment in relation to human diseases, and to consider briefly the implications for the means of their control. Diseases and disabilities can be divided broadly into four classes as follows.

CONDITIONS DETERMINED AT FERTILIZATION

(*a*) *Genetic diseases.* This term is interpreted to include both single gene disorders, which are simply inherited, and chromosomal aberrations which are largely eliminated as abortions. Genetic diseases, so defined, are uncommon among abnormalities manifested at birth or in post-natal life.

(*b*) *Other diseases determined at fertilization.* These comprise mainly conditions associated with the genetically programmed wearing-out of organs at the end of life. They are not simply inherited, but are attributable to multiple genes which are nevertheless highly specific.

CONDITIONS WHICH OCCUR ONLY IN AN APPROPRIATE ENVIRONMENT

(*c*) *Diseases in which the environmental influences are prenatal.* These include most abortions and stillbirths, congenital abnormalities (such as malformations and most cases of mental subnormality) and some conditions which first come to attention in post-natal life (most non-infective disorders of childhood are determined by the time of birth). These diseases are attributable to unknown influences within the uterus operating on genetic material whose character is also obscure.

(*d*) *Diseases in which the environmental influences are post-natal.* They comprise conditions, both infective and non-infective, which, so far as is known, are not due to influences before birth. They probably include nearly all the common diseases and disabilities (accidents, diabetes, peptic ulcer, rheumatoid arthritis, psychiatric disorders, etc.) as well as others such as the cancers which formerly would have been attributed to inborn constitution (class (*b*) above). They are usually described as multifactorial, which tells us little more than that their aetiology is complex and their genetic basis obscure.

I shall examine the implications of this classification more closely in Chapter 6, but three comments should be made at this point. One is that diseases in the first three classes are all relatively intractable, but for quite different reasons: the first two because they are determined at fertilization, and the third because environmental influences during pregnancy are difficult to recognize and control. Second, the age trend of mortality in the past century is what would be expected from the classification: little improvement before birth and a large reduction post-natally, mainly in younger age-groups, brought about by a decline of deaths from diseases in the fourth class. And third, in principle all the diseases in the fourth class could be prevented by appropriate environmental modifications; but in practice control of infections is often relatively simple, whereas control of non-communicable diseases may be complex and may require public or private decisions which are difficult to accept.

3

Diseases which
have declined

Although the documentary evidence was very unsatisfactory
before births and deaths were registered nationally, there is no
doubt that there has been a vast improvement in health during the
past three centuries. During most of man's existence it is probable
that a considerable proportion of all children died or were killed
within a few years of birth; in technologically advanced countries
today, more than 95 per cent survive to adult life. To interpret the
influences which have been responsible for this remarkable increase in expectation of life it is necessary to identify the diseases
associated with the decline of mortality.

Although births, deaths, and population size were recorded
earlier in some other countries (in Sweden from the mid eighteenth
century), cause of death was registered first in England and Wales
(in 1838). In the years immediately after registration the data were
incomplete or for other reasons unsatisfactory, but from 1841 it is
possible to examine the trend of mortality associated with specific
diseases. These records from the nineteenth century are of in-
estimable value; they are not available elsewhere, so in other countries interpretation is virtually restricted to the twentieth century.
This may explain the frequent overestimation of the contribution
of immunization and therapy, since these measures have had their
impact mainly, indeed with one exception wholly, since 1900.

THE TREND OF MORTALITY

Fig. 3.1 shows the death-rate for males and females from 1841 to
1971. For the nineteenth century the rates for the six decades were
standardized to correspond to the age of the population of 1901;
for the twentieth century the rates are for the first year of each
decade, again standardized in relation to the 1901 population.
Standardization is needed to correct for the changing age structure,

FIGURE 3.1. Death rates (standardized to 1901 population):
England and Wales.

since with an ageing population the crude death-rates under-estimate the reduction of mortality which actually occurred. Throughout the period death-rates were considerably higher for males than for females; they began to fall in the eighth decade of the nineteenth century and the decline has continued to the present day.

However the examination cannot be restricted to the post-registration period, since the enormous growth of population (in England and Wales it trebled between 1700 and 1851) leaves no doubt that the decline of the death-rate began well before 1838. Table 3.1 shows the proportion of the reduction of mortality

Determinants of health

TABLE 3.1. *Reduction of mortality since 1700: England and Wales.*

Period	Percentage of total reduction in each period*	Percentage of reduction due to infections
1700 to 1848–54	33	?
1848–54 to 1901	20	92
1901 to 1971	47	73
1700 to 1971	100	

*The estimates are based on the assumption that the death-rate in 1700 was 30.

which occurred in three periods: 1700 to the mid nineteenth century (33 per cent); the second half of the nineteenth century (20 per cent); and the twentieth century (47 per cent). These figures are based on the assumption that the death-rate in England and Wales at the beginning of the eighteenth century was 30. The Swedish death-rate for the period 1751 to 1800 was 27·4 and the rate for England and Wales is believed to have been at about the same level or a little higher.

Table 3.1 also shows the proportion of the decline of mortality that was associated with infectious diseases: 92 per cent in 1848–54 to 1901; and 73 per cent in 1901 to 1971. On the assumption that there was no decrease of non-infective deaths in the pre-registration period, 86 per cent of the total reduction of the death-rate, from the beginning of the eighteenth century to the present day, was attributable to the decline of the infections.

DISEASES ASSOCIATED WITH THE DECLINE OF MORTALITY IN THE POST-REGISTRATION PERIOD

From 1838, or a little after, the contribution of different diseases to the reduction of mortality can be followed from the Registrar-General's statistics. There are of course many problems which arise from vagueness and inaccuracy of diagnosis and from changes in nomenclature and classification. For example there must be doubts about the diagnosis of tuberculosis at a time when it was not possible to X-ray the chest or identify the tubercle bacillus. Scarlet fever was not separated from diphtheria in the national classification until 1855 nor typhus from typhoid until 1869. In spite of such difficulties, when handled critically the

31

Registrar-General's data can be used to identify the diseases associated with the decline of the death-rate during the nineteenth and twentieth centuries.

In the discussion which follows conditions attributable to micro-organisms will be distinguished from conditions which are not. The distinction cannot be made in all cases. For example, in the early post-registration period rheumatic heart disease was not separated from other diseases of the heart; so, although it is caused by streptococcal infection, it is included with other diseases of the heart among conditions not due to micro-organisms. In the early period nephritis was classified with dropsy which is partly of non-infective origin, so when data for the mid nineteenth century are used nephritis is included with conditions not attributable to micro-organisms, although most cases result from bacterial infection. There are a few other infective conditions which even today cannot be separated in national statistics, for example diseases of the heart and nervous system due to syphilis and congenital malformations which result from rubella. With these reservations, the broad distinction between infective and non-infective conditions can be made with reasonable confidence.

CONDITIONS ATTRIBUTABLE TO MICRO-ORGANISMS

Table 3.2 shows the reduction of mortality between 1848–54 and 1971 associated with infectious diseases in three groups: airborne; water- and food-borne; and other. The years 1848–54 have been taken to represent the beginning of the post-registration period because certification of cause of death was incomplete during part of the first decade after registration, and the rates for 1848–54 and 1971 were standardized to correspond with the age distribution of the 1901 population. Of the fall of mortality which has occurred since the mid nineteenth century, 40 per cent was from airborne diseases, 21 per cent from water- and food-borne diseases, 13 per cent from other infections, and the remainder (26 per cent) from non-infective conditions.

Airborne diseases. Table 3.3 shows the contribution made by different airborne diseases to the total decline of mortality between 1848–54 and 1971. Respiratory tuberculosis accounted for

TABLE 3.2. *Reduction of mortality, 1848–54 to 1971: England and Wales.*

	Percentage of reduction
Conditions attributable to micro-organisms	
1. Airborne disease	40
2. Water- and food-borne diseases	21
3. Other conditions	13
Total	74
Conditions not attributable to micro-organisms	26
All diseases	100

The estimate of the proportion of deaths associated with micro-organisms is lower than would be suggested by Table 3.1, because when the whole period (1848–54 to 1971) is considered, certain infections (for example rheumatic fever) cannot be included.

TABLE 3.3. *Standardized death-rates (per million) from airborne diseases: England and Wales.*

	1848–54	1971	Percentage of reduction from all causes attributable to each disease
Tuberculosis (respiratory)	2,901	13	17·5
Bronchitis, pneumonia, influenza	2,239	603	9·9
Whooping cough	423	1	2·6
Measles	342	0	2·1
Scarlet fever and diphtheria	1,016	0	6·2
Smallpox	263	0	1·6
Infections of ear, pharynx, larynx	75	2	0·4
Total	7,259	619	40·3

17.5 per cent, and more than half of this improvement occurred before the end of the nineteenth century. Mortality from the disease fell continuously, at least from the time when cause of death was first registered, and by the fifth decade it had fallen by about a quarter.

The next largest contribution was from bronchitis, pneumonia, and influenza (9·9 per cent). It is unfortunately necessary to group these conditions because there is some evidence of transfers from one to another. For example, both pneumonia and bronchitis deaths show an increase in years of high influenza prevalence, and it seems clear that a number of influenza deaths were ascribed wrongly to pneumonia, and, even more frequently, to bronchitis. Confusion between bronchitis and pneumonia, at least in old people, is suggested by the fact that the death-rate of men aged 75 and over attributed to pneumonia increased between 1901 and 1971, whereas deaths from bronchitis decreased. It is also possible that some deaths which earlier would have been certified as 'old age' were transferred to this category, in which case the number of deaths from these respiratory diseases would have been larger in 1901 and the decline by 1971 correspondingly greater. The trend of mortality will be examined more closely later, but here it should be said that there is evidence that the reduction of the death-rate from pneumonia, bronchitis, and influenza began before the end of the nineteenth century. This was the conclusion reached about pneumonia by Magill: 'the rapid decline of pneumonia death rates began in New York State before the turn of the century and many years before the "miracle" drugs were known'.[1]

Diphtheria and scarlet fever were associated with 6·2 per cent of the fall of mortality (from 1848–54 to 1971) and three-fifths of this decline occurred before 1901. The diseases can be separated after 1855; the death-rate from scarlet fever fell rapidly in the second half of the nineteenth century, whereas that from diphtheria increased slightly. Since 1901 both have declined, and there have been few deaths from either disease in England and Wales since 1951.

Whooping cough contributed 2·6 per cent to the reduction of mortality. The decrease was relatively small in the nineteenth century and accounted for only about a quarter of the fall between 1848–54 and 1971. Nevertheless mortality from the disease has declined almost continuously since about 1870, and there are now few deaths in England and Wales (26 in 1971, of which 22 were in children under 1 year).

Measles was associated with 2·1 per cent of the fall of the death-rate between 1848–54 and 1971. During the nineteenth and early twentieth centuries childhood mortality from measles was

1. Magill, T. P., 'The immunologist and the evil spirits', *Journal of Immunology*, **74** (1955), p. 1.

TABLE 3.4. *Standardized death-rates (per million) from water- and food-borne diseases: England and Wales.*

	1848–54	1971	Percentage of reduction from all causes attributable to each disease
Cholera, diarrhoea, dysentery	1,819	33	10·8
Tuberculosis (non-respiratory)	753	2	4·6
Typhoid, typhus	990	0	6·0
Total	3,562	35	21·4

relatively high, but it fell rapidly from about the time of the First World War. Nevertheless measles remains an important disease; in 1971, 135,000 cases were notified and there were 28 deaths.

Smallpox contributed 1·6 per cent to the reduction of the death-rate and almost all of this improvement occurred before 1901. Since about 1910 there have been few deaths from smallpox in the British Isles.

It seems unnecessary to comment in detail on the remaining infections (of the ear, pharynx, and larynx), which accounted for only 0·4 per cent of the fall of mortality. There are also some airborne diseases which caused few deaths and have been classified under 'other conditions'.

Water- and food-borne diseases. Water- and food-borne diseases (Table 3.4) were associated with about a fifth of the fall of the death-rate between 1848–54 and 1971; nearly half of the improvement occurred before 1901.

It seems desirable to group together the diarrhoeal diseases. In the twentieth century they comprised essentially diarrhoea, dysentery, and enteritis; but in the period 1848–54 there was also a considerable number of deaths attributed to cholera which are therefore included under the same heading. These diseases were responsible for about a tenth of the fall in mortality before 1971; a third of the decline occurred before 1901.

Deaths associated with non-respiratory tuberculosis in 1848–54 are those shown in the Registrar-General's classification as scrofula, *tabes mesenteri,* and hydrocephalus. Deaths attributed to hydrocephalus include some due to the congenital and other forms of the disease; however, in the nineteenth century most deaths were undoubtedly from tuberculous meningitis, and since the different types were not then separated in national statistics, it seems right to classify them with other forms of non-respiratory tuberculosis. This overstatement of non-respiratory tuberculosis deaths is compensated by the inevitable omission of deaths due to renal and bone and joint tuberculosis. From 1901 the classification was reasonably comprehensive, and there is little difficulty in following the trend of mortality from that time. The disease was responsible for 4·6 per cent of the reduction of the death-rate between 1848–54 and 1971 and about a quarter of the improvement occurred before 1901.

Since typhus was not distinguished from typhoid fever before 1869, they are considered together in Table 3.4. It is unfortunate that this grouping is necessary, since typhus is not spread by water and food and should be included under 'other conditions'. The balance of deaths due to typhus and typhoid before 1869 is uncertain, but from that time at least the latter greatly outnumbered the former. The death-rate from typhus fell rapidly in the last decade of the nineteenth century and there have been few deaths during the twentieth. Together these diseases were associated with 6 per cent of the reduction of mortality between 1848–54 and 1971, of which 84 per cent occurred before 1901.

It should be noted that the rate of decline of mortality before the turn of the century was much greater for the enteric diseases, spread mainly by water, than for the diarrhoeal diseases spread mainly by food.

Other diseases due to micro-organisms. There remains a miscellaneous group of conditions of infective origin, which are not spread mainly by air, water, or food, or for which certification of cause of death was unsatisfactory (as in the case of 'convulsions and teething'). Diseases of this class were responsible for 12·6 per cent of the fall of mortality between 1848–54 and 1971 and about a third of this decrease occurred before 1901.

36

TABLE 3.5. *Standardized death-rates (per million) for other diseases attributable to micro-organisms: England and Wales.*

	1848–54	1971	Percentage of reduction from all causes attributable to each disease
Convulsions, teething	1,322	0	8·0
Syphilis	50	0	0·3
Appendicitis, peritonitis	75	7	0·4
Puerperal fever	62	1	0·4
Other infections	635	52	3·5
Total	2,144	60	12·6

Table 3.5 shows the contribution made by different conditions; the largest (8 per cent) was from convulsions and teething. Although these terms were long regarded as unsatisfactory, they were still employed in 1901 when 20,956 deaths were attributed to them. By 1911 the term teething was no longer accepted, although it was still used in association with convulsions. The use of convulsions also diminished; only 9 deaths were so certified in 1961 and none in 1971. This decrease was presumably due mainly to transfer of deaths to other and more acceptable causes, as well as to the general decline of the underlying infections.

Most of these deaths were infective. They were associated particularly with diseases of childhood (whooping cough, measles, otitis media, meningitis, pneumonia, gastro-enteritis, etc.), and in this analysis attention has been restricted to deaths under 5 years in the Registrar-General's reports. Although it is not possible to identify the causes of death included under convulsions and teething, it is probable that most of them were airborne infections.

The other diseases specified in Table 3.5 contributed little to the decline of mortality: syphilis, 0·3 per cent; appendicitis and peritonitis, 0·4 per cent; and puerperal fever, 0·4 per cent. Except in the case of appendicitis there are no special difficulties in identifying these conditions in the Registrar-General's classification. Syphilis is taken to include the principal manifestations of the disease: general paralysis of the insane, locomotor ataxia, and aneurysm. Until 1951 the frequency of deaths from cardiovascular syphilis was slightly understated, because the classification did not separate those due to syphilitic valvular disease. Until 1931 the number of deaths attributed to puerperal fever was also somewhat low because infective deaths associated with abortion were not identified.

CONDITIONS NOT ATTRIBUTABLE TO MICRO-ORGANISMS

The conditions under this heading (Table 3.6) are a heterogeneous collection, having in common only that they are not due to micro-organisms or, in a few cases where they are, that they cannot be identified in national statistics. Together these conditions were associated with 25·6 per cent of the decline of mortality since 1848–54 and a tenth of this reduction occurred before 1901.

TABLE 3.6. *Standardized death-rates (per million) from conditions not attributable to micro-organisms: England and Wales.*

	1848–54	1971	Percentage of reduction from all causes attributable to each condition
Congenital defects	28	127	0·6 increase
Prematurity, immaturity, other diseases of infancy	1,221	192	6·2
Cerebrovascular disease	890	603	1·7
Rheumatic heart disease	64	88	0·1 increase
Other cardiovascular disease	634	1,688	6·4 increase
Cancer	307	1,169	5·2 increase
Other diseases of digestive system	706	105	3·6
Other diseases of nervous system	316	63	1·5
Nephritis	615	46	3·5
Other diseases of urinary system	107	23	0·5
Pregnancy and childbirth (excluding sepsis)	130	3	0·8
Violence	761	345	2·5
Old age	1,447	16	8·7
Other diseases	1,665	202	8·9
Total	8,891	4,670	25·6

There are many problems of terminology and classification. For example, the term 'old age' was common, and although it was recognized to be unsatisfactory more than a fifth of the deaths of persons aged 65 and over were attributed to it in 1901. From 1911 the use of the term diminished, deaths presumably being transferred to more acceptable causes, both infectious (for example pneumonia) and non-infectious (heart disease). This category of deaths contributed 8·7 per cent to the decline.

The heading 'prematurity, immaturity, and other diseases of infancy', associated with 6·2 per cent of the decline, undoubtedly covers a large number of very different conditions. As knowledge of neonatal diseases increased, the classification was expanded, and some deaths were transferred to more satisfactory categories. However, these distinctions cannot be made in the nineteenth and early twentieth centuries, so it is necessary to combine prematurity with other diseases of infancy. Deaths in this class increased in the late nineteenth century, and did not decline until 1901. This largely accounts for the delay in the fall of infant mortality.

Difficulties arise with 'other diseases of the nervous system'. For example, poliomyelitis was not specified in the 1901 and 1911 classifications, and was probably grouped with 'diseases of the cord' which therefore include a few infective deaths. However, the error is small, for poliomyelitis was not then or later a common cause of death. Paralysis agitans did not appear in 1901 and 1911, but has been included since 1921 although some cases are believed to result from virus infection. This may be true also of multiple sclerosis, shown separately from 1921.

These examples, which could be extended, are characteristic of the problems of terminology and classification which arise with conditions not attributable to micro-organisms. There is a further difficulty. In the case of the infections the division according to mode of transmission will facilitate interpretation of reasons for their decline. No such approach is possible in the case of non-infective causes of death. For example, cancer mortality has increased during this century; this increase is mainly the result of deaths from lung cancer caused by smoking, and it has masked a fall of mortality from some other cancers, brought about by therapy and, no doubt, other influences. The picture is also complex in cardiovascular disease, where a large increase in deaths from myocardial infarction may have obscured a reduction from other forms. The contribution of treatment in cases of violence is probably understated because of an increase in the frequency of severe injuries.

It should be noted that the reduction of mortality was lower for males than for females (21·3 per cent and 31·6 per cent respectively in the twentieth century). This sex difference is due partly to the increase in male deaths from lung cancer and cardiovascular disease, without which the fall in male mortality from non-infectious deaths would have been much larger. This means that the decline of mortality for male non-smokers has been considerably greater than the figures suggest.

DISEASES ASSOCIATED WITH THE DECLINE OF MORTALITY IN THE PRE-REGISTRATION PERIOD

INFECTIONS

With the probable exceptions of infanticide and starvation (discussed below), the fall of mortality before registration, as in the period from registration to 1900, was almost certainly due to a reduction of deaths from infectious diseases. As a preliminary to interpretation of the reasons for this reduction, it is desirable to come to a conclusion about the nature of the diseases which declined. For the pre-registration period there are no reliable data concerning individual diseases, so one must draw largely on later experience.

From 1838 the infections which declined were mainly of two types: airborne, and water- and food-borne. Mortality from some of the airborne infections, particularly tuberculosis, fell from the time of registration but the decline from water- and food-borne diseases was delayed until the last decades of the nineteenth century.

It is probable that there was a substantial reduction of mortality from airborne infections in the pre-registration period. The number of deaths from tuberculosis fell rapidly from 1838, and the disease was associated with nearly half of the decrease of the death-rate during the second half of the nineteenth century. Mortality from tuberculosis was considerable in the seventeenth and eighteenth centuries, and the fact that it was declining at the time of registration suggests that it may have fallen earlier.

Another airborne infection from which deaths must have decreased before 1838 is smallpox. In 1848–54 the death-rate from the disease was only 263 (per million), less than a tenth of the rate for respiratory tuberculosis and considerably lower than the rates from whooping cough and measles (Table 3.3). We can be less confident about the trend of mortality from other airborne infections in the pre-registration period. Diphtheria was confused with scarlet fever and there is no reliable information about deaths from diseases such as whooping cough, measles, bronchitis, pneumonia, and influenza.

Evidence concerning water- and food-borne diseases is also lacking. Mortality was not falling in the decades after registration, and did not begin to decline until there were improvements in water and sewage disposal, in England and Wales from the seventh decade. Indeed the expansion of populations and the rapid movement from country to towns must have increased exposure to infections spread by water and food, and the appearance of cholera, possibly for the first time, indicates that hygienic conditions deteriorated.

Finally, I must consider the possible significance of the vector-borne diseases (plague, typhus, and malaria) spread by rats, lice, and mosquitoes. These diseases were relatively unimportant after registration: plague almost disappeared from the British Isles after 1679, and although cases were introduced occasionally through seaports, no extension of the disease occurred; typhus was not separated from typhoid in national statistics before 1869 and few deaths were attributed to it after that time; and although there may have been some indigenous cases of malaria, most deaths have resulted from infections acquired overseas.

If judged by the attention paid to it by historians, plague was much the most important of the vector-borne diseases in relation to the decline of mortality and growth of population in earlier centuries. However, since the disease virtually disappeared after 1679, it cannot have been associated with the decrease of deaths from 1700.

41

Typhus was not differentiated from bubonic plague until about the middle of the nineteenth century and was probably responsible for many of the deaths attributed to that disease. As already mentioned, typhus was also confused with typhoid. Malaria could not be identified reliably from many other fevers before the late nineteenth century, and in the early Registrar-General's reports it was presumably included under terms such as intermittent fever. In view of the lack of evidence one can attempt only a personal appraisal. I suggest that there were epidemics of typhus, particularly affecting the poor, at intervals during the pre-registration period, and that mortality declined until the disease virtually disappeared in the late nineteenth century; that malaria was never an important cause of death in Britain (where climatic conditions are not really suited to the parasite) and the disease was not associated significantly with the reduction of mortality in the pre-registration period.

In this assessment, vector-borne diseases are assigned a much less significant place in the history of mortality than the one they occupy in developing countries today. The reason is clear. Most developing countries are in or near the tropics, where climatic conditions are ideal for many parasites and animal vectors: particularly flies, mosquitoes, and snails, with the result that diseases such as dysentery, malaria, yellow fever, and bilharzia are endemic over large areas. But in western Europe, even in past centuries conditions were unsuitable for nearly all diseases spread by animal vectors. For example, a temperature of not less than 20° C is required before the sexual cycle of *Plasmodium falciparum* (the cause of malignant subtertian malaria) can be completed in the mosquito, and a temperature of 15° is needed for other species. For this reason it is unlikely that malaria was ever common in Britain.

NON-INFECTIVE CONDITIONS

Table 3.1 suggested that in the period from 1848–54 to 1901, non-infective conditions were associated with 8 per cent of the decline of mortality. Most of this reduction was in two classes of deaths, 'old age' and 'other diseases', neither of which provides convincing evidence of a decline. The term old age was used in respect of both infectious and non-infectious deaths, and the fact that in this period there was a considerable increase of deaths certified as bronchitis, pneumonia and influenza, and other cardiovascular diseases, suggests that the apparent fall in old age deaths resulted mainly from a transfer to these categories. The other diseases comprised a large and heterogeneous group of conditions, many of which were unsatisfactorily classified (for example haemorrhage, mortification, and insanity). Moreover, the reduction of deaths was mainly in two categories. One consisted of 'asthma and diseases of lungs, etc.'. Many of the deaths attributed to these causes were probably associated with respiratory infections, and the apparent decline between 1848–54 and 1901 may have been due mainly to transfers to other categories (such as bronchitis, pneumonia, and influenza) as a result of improved certification. The other class of deaths which fell substantially was 'debility, atrophy and sudden death, cause unknown'. The first two of these terms are quite unsatisfactory and the reduction of deaths was no doubt due largely to improvements in diagnosis and classification. Although violent deaths are shown separately in the Registrar-General's reports, those classified as sudden deaths may have included a considerable number caused by violence. About a quarter of these deaths were in the first year of life, so that some may have been due to infanticide. Others, no doubt, were similar to those which would be described today as cot deaths, which means that the cause of death was unknown.

Against this background it seems reasonable to conclude that the Registrar-General's statistics provide no convincing evidence of a reduction of deaths from non-infective causes between 1848–54 and 1901, and the estimate of 8 per cent (Table 3.1) is probably due mainly to errors of certification.

It would seem to follow that the fall of mortality in the pre-registration period was associated almost entirely with infectious diseases. However, there are two non-infective causes of death (infanticide and starvation) which may have been important, although this cannot be confirmed from national statistics.

In a survey of the history of infanticide, Langer concluded that it was practised on a substantial scale in both ancient and modern times.[1] In the eighteenth and nineteenth centuries, 'the poor, hardly able to support the family they already had, evaded responsibility by disposing of further additions'. The same conclusion was reached by many contemporary writers, among them Disraeli who believed that infanticide 'was hardly less prevalent in England than on the banks of the Ganges'. Langer also quoted Ryan who examined the medico-legal aspects of the problem of infanticide: 'We cannot ignore the fact that the crime of infanticide, as well as that of criminal abortion, is widespread and on the increase.' Although there is no means of estimating the frequency of infanticide, there seems no reason to dissent from Langer's view that it was common until the last quarter of the nineteenth century, when it began to be reduced by stringent regulations, by growing public interest in maternal and child care, and finally and most effectively, by the spread of contraceptive practices.

It is also impossible to assess the frequency of death from starvation, as distinct from death from infectious diseases which resulted from poor nutrition. Although experience in developing countries today suggests that the latter was much more common than the former, it seems probable that in the eighteenth and nineteenth centuries death did occur, at times not infrequently, as a direct result of food deficiency. In the first full year of registration of cause of death, 167 deaths were attributed to starvation. However, an analysis of 63 deaths by Farr showed that the classification was unsatisfactory (they included 12 persons who died from the effects of cold).

In spite of the lack of statistical evidence, I believe it is permissible to conclude that death from infanticide was probably common, and death from starvation not uncommon, in the eighteenth and nineteenth centuries. If this is true, mortality from these causes may have declined before registration of cause of death in 1838, and certainly did so after that time. Although this trend cannot be confirmed from national statistics, it is quite possible that these were the only non-infective causes of death associated with a significant reduction of mortality before the twentieth century.

1. Langer, W. L., 'Infanticide: a historical survey', *History of Childhood Quarterly*, I (1974), p. 353.

4

Infectious diseases

In Chapter 3 it was concluded that the fall of mortality since the end of the seventeenth century was due predominantly to a reduction of deaths from infectious diseases. However, non-infective causes of death were associated with about a quarter of the decrease of deaths in this century. To understand the influences which have brought about the modern improvement in health it is therefore necessary to examine the reasons for the decline of the infections and of certain non-infective conditions. These are the subjects which will be discussed in this chapter and the one that follows.

This brings us to an important question in the history of the past three centuries: It is probable that the predominance of infectious diseases dates from the first agricultural revolution when men began to aggregate in populations of considerable size: Why then did the infections decline from about the time of the modern agricultural and industrial revolutions which led to the aggregation of still larger and more densely packed populations? The answer to this paradox must be sought in the character of micro-organisms, the conditions under which they spread and the response of the human host, inherited or acquired.

However, for an understanding of the infections it is unsatisfactory to consider separately an organism and its host. They are living things which interact and adapt to each other by natural selection. The virulence of an organism is not, therefore, a distinct character like its size or shape: it is an expression of an interaction between a particular organism and a particular host. For example, a measles virus whose effects on children in a developed country are relatively benign, may have devastating effects when encountered by a population for the first time. When assessing the major influences on the infections it will therefore be necessary to distinguish between the following:

Infectious diseases

(a) Interaction between organism and host. When exposed to
micro-organisms over a period of time, the hosts gain through
natural selection an intrinsic resistance which is genetically determined. In addition to this intrinsic resistance immunity may also be
acquired, by transmission from the mother or in response to a
post-natal infection. These types of immunity, inherited and
acquired, are not due to either medical intervention or, as a rule,
to identifiable environmental influences.

(b) Immunization and therapy. Immunity may also result from
successful immunization, and the outcome of an established infection may be modified by therapy.

(c) Modes of spread. Modes of spread are very different for
different micro-organisms, and the feasibility of control by preventing contact with an organism is determined largely by the
way it is transmitted. In a developed country it is relatively easy to
stop the spread of cholera by purification of water; it is more
difficult to control salmonella infection by supervision of food-
handling; and at present it is impossible to eliminate an airborne
infection such as the common cold by preventing exposure to the
virus.

(d) The nutrition of the host. The results of an encounter with a
micro-organism are influenced not only by the inherited or
acquired immunity of the host, but also by his general state of
health determined particularly, it will be suggested, by nutrition.

This classification provides a basis for an analysis of reasons for
the decline of infectious diseases. It is against the background of an
understanding of the interaction between organism and host that
we must consider the possibility that the decline was due substantially to a change in the character of the diseases, essentially
independent of both medical intervention and identifiable environmental (including nutritional) improvements. It is in relation
to immunization and therapy that we must assess the contribution
of specific medical measures. A judgement on the significance of
reduction of exposure to infection must rest on understanding
of the modes of spread of micro-organisms. And an estimate of
the importance of an increase in food supplies requires appraisal
of the association between malnutrition and infection.

46

A CHANGE IN THE CHARACTER OF INFECTIOUS DISEASES

Was the decline of the infections during the past few centuries associated with a change in the character of the diseases, that is, with modification of the relation between micro-organisms and their hosts? Such a change is not independent of the environment; indeed it is determined largely by an ecological relationship to the environment. It is, however, of a kind which must have occurred continuously during man's history, essentially independent both of medical intervention, and of measures such as better hygiene and improved nutrition.

Some biologists have suggested that a change of this type was important, and even that it was the main reason for the decline of mortality and improvement in health. In his presidential address to the American Association of Immunologists in 1954 Magill wrote: 'It would seem to be a more logical conclusion that during recent years, quite regardless of our therapeutic efforts, a state of relative equilibrium has established itself between the microbes and the "ever-varying state of the immunological constitution of the herd"—a relative equilibrium which will continue, perhaps, just as long as it is not disturbed, unduly, by biological events.'[1] According to this interpretation, the trend of mortality from infectious diseases has been essentially independent of both medical measures and the vast economic and social developments of the past three centuries.

The grounds on which it was possible to reach so radical a conclusion are important. Magill based his views on the ineffectiveness and dangers of vaccination against rabies, the decline of tuberculosis long before effective treatment, the behaviour of diphtheria in the nineteenth century (it increased in prevalence and malignancy in the middle of the century and declined before the introduction of antitoxin), and the rapid reduction of pneumonia death-rates in New York State before the 'miracle' drugs were known, followed by an arrest of the decline from about the time when antibiotics were introduced. Moreover, these examples could be extended: the cholera vaccine required until recently by

1. Magill, T. P., 'The immunologist and the evil spirits', *Journal of Immunology*, **74** (1955), 1.

international regulations, is almost useless; the reduction of mortality from diphtheria in the 1940s did not everywhere coincide with the introduction of immunization; and scarlet fever has had a variable history which appears to have been independent of medical and other influences.

Nevertheless, although specific measures may have had little effect on the behaviour of many infections, the question concerning the significance of changes in the character of the infectious diseases is complex. It will therefore be desirable to examine the implications of the suggestion that the decline of mortality was due substantially to a favourable change in the 'ever-varying state of the immunological constitution of the herd'.

The immunological constitution of a generation is influenced largely by the mortality experience of those which precede it. This was particularly true in past centuries, when the majority of liveborn people died from infectious diseases without reproducing. Under such conditions there was rigorous natural selection in respect of immunity to infection. The proposal that the decline of mortality resulted from a change in the immunological constitution of the population therefore implies that there was heavy mortality at an earlier period which led to the birth of individuals who were genetically less susceptible. According to this interpretation, the substantial and prolonged decline of infectious deaths was due largely, not to improvements since the eighteenth century, but to an earlier deterioration of conditions which led to the high mortality which must have preceded it.

AIRBORNE DISEASES

Although there is no airborne infection, indeed there is no infection, of which one can say that there has been no change in the relation between the organism and host since the eighteenth century, there are some such as tuberculosis and, probably, measles in which this is unlikely to be the main reason for the decrease of deaths. But the objection to this as the major influence on all airborne infections is of a more general kind. To believe that the reduction of deaths from these diseases was due essentially to a change in their character, we should have to accept either (*a*) that fortuitously, over the whole range of airborne diseases, there was

48

a change of the kind which appears to have occurred in scarlet fever, independent of medical or other recognizable influences, or (*b*) that certain deleterious influences led to high mortality in the eighteenth century, which, through natural selection, resulted in the survival of more resistant populations. In the light of the extent and duration of the fall of mortality the first explanation is incredible. And since there is no evidence that mortality from infectious diseases increased greatly in the eighteenth century (on the contrary, there is indirect evidence that it declined) the second explanation is equally untenable.

WATER- AND FOOD-BORNE DISEASES

Some of the issues are analogous to those discussed above: the relation of the organisms to their hosts is variable, so that over any considerable period there are changes in the diseases; and where there is high mortality natural selection results in more resistant populations. Is it likely that this was a significant influence on the reduction of deaths from water- and food-borne diseases in the late nineteenth century?

Although living conditions must have deteriorated in the first half of the century, it is most unlikely that this was a major influence on the subsequent decline of mortality. In the first place, there is no evidence of a large increase of deaths from the diseases; and secondly, another and more plausible explanation is available, namely, improvements in hygiene (discussed below). This illustrates the advantages of examining water- and food-borne infections separately from those that are airborne. A change in the character of airborne diseases has to be considered in the light of the fact that exposure to the organisms cannot be prevented. But in the case of water- and food-borne diseases, separation from the source of infection was the critical step in their control. While, therefore, we cannot exclude the possibility that typhoid and dysentery at the end of the nineteenth century differed somewhat from the same diseases in the early industrial towns, it is unlikely that any difference was a major reason for the rapid decline of mortality from intestinal infections which followed improvements in water supply and sewage disposal.

VECTOR-BORNE DISEASES

As already noted, typhus is the vector-borne disease which may have contributed significantly to the fall of mortality in Britain, mainly in the eighteenth and early nineteenth centuries. As in the case of other epidemic infections, knowledge of the multiple factors which led to its disappearance and reappearance is still incomplete; but we cannot rule out the possibility that they included a change in the character of the disease, apparently unrelated to medical measures or identifiable environmental influences. However, even if the decrease of deaths from typhus could be accounted for largely in this way, its contribution to the decline of mortality would have been very small.

I conclude that the reduction of deaths from infectious diseases was not due substantially to a change in their character. This is not to suggest that it has not been modified, except in the case of scarlet fever and a few other less clear-cut examples. On the contrary, it is possible that genetically determined resistance to diseases such as tuberculosis and typhoid is lower today than it was in the eighteenth and nineteenth centuries. But if so, this has come about as a secondary consequence of reduced exposure, rather than through a primary change in the relation between the organisms and man. Moreover it is a change which, acting independently, would be expected to increase mortality rather than to reduce it.

IMMUNIZATION AND THERAPY

Until recently it was accepted, almost without question, that the modern improvement in health was due essentially to medical measures. However this term is often used loosely in relation to both personal medical care and public health services; and since we are concerned here with the contribution of immunization and therapy (rather than our indebtedness to medical science in all its forms), it is important to distinguish between the two.

AIRBORNE DISEASES

It is in respect of airborne diseases that assessment of the contribution of immunization and therapy is most important because (*a*) they were associated with the largest reduction of the death-rate (40·3 per cent) between 1848–54 and 1971 and (*b*) there is another obvious explanation for the decline of the water- and food-borne diseases which also contributed substantially.

Table 4.1 gives (in the second column) the proportion of the fall of the standardized death-rate associated with each disease or, in two cases, disease group. The table also shows the years when specific measures were introduced. The procedures referred to are as follows.

Tuberculosis: streptomycin, 1947. It is now well recognized that the methods of treatment in the first half of this century, for example pneumothorax and thorocoplasty, were of little value. The general use of BCG vaccination began later, in 1954.

Bronchitis, pneumonia, and influenza: sulphapyridine, 1938. Specific measures were ineffective before the introduction of the sulphonamides. The earliest (prontosil and sulphanilamide) were effective only against the streptococcus but trials of sulphapyridine suggested that it reduced mortality from lobar pneumonia. The scope of treatment was extended by the antibiotics which became available for civilian use about 1945.

Whooping cough: sulphonamides, 1938. Even today the effect of treatment by sulphonamides and antibiotics on the course of the disease is questionable. Immunization was used widely from 1952; the protective effect is variable, and has been estimated to lie between less than 20 per cent and more than 80 per cent.

Measles: sulphonamides, 1935. Effective specific measures have only recently become available in the form of immunization and they had no significant effect on the trend of the death-rate. However, mortality from the disease is due largely to invasion by secondary organisms which have been treated by chemotherapy since 1935.

Scarlet fever: sulphonamides, 1935. There was no effective treatment before the introduction of prontosil.

Diphtheria: antitoxin, 1894. Antitoxin was used from the late nineteenth century and has been the accepted form of treatment since that time. Although questions have been raised about its

TABLE 4.1. Airborne diseases: fall of mortality since introduction of specific measures of prophylaxis or treatment: England and Wales.

Cause	Fall in standardized death-rate between 1848–54 and 1971 (a)	Fall as percentage of fall from all causes (b)	Year when specific measures became available	Fall by 1971 after introduction of specific measures (c)	Proportion of total fall after introduction of specific measures $\frac{c}{a}$	Fall after introduction of specific measures as percentage of total fall from all causes bc/a
Tuberculosis (respiratory)	2,888	17·5	1947	409	0·14	2·5
Bronchitis, pneumonia, influenza	1,636	9·9	1938	531	0·32	3·2
Whooping cough	422	2·6	1938	43	0·10	0·3
Measles	342	2·1	1935	50	0·15	0·3
Scarlet fever	1,016	6·2	1935	15 } 292	0·30	1·9
Diphtheria			1894			
Smallpox	263	1·6	Before 1848	263	1·00	1·6
Infections of ear, pharynx, larynx	73	0·4	1935	65	0·89	0·4
	6,640	40·3	–	1,668	0·25	10·1

effectiveness, it is generally believed to have lowered the case fatality rate, which fell from 8·2 per 100 notifications in 1916–25 to 5·4 in 1933–42, while notifications remained at an average level above 50,000 per year. The mortality rate increased at the beginning of the last war, but fell rapidly from about the time when national immunization was introduced.

Smallpox: vaccination, before 1848–54.

Infections of ear, pharynx, and larynx: sulphonamides, 1935. The main therapeutic influences have been chemotherapy and, in some ear infections, surgery. It is difficult to say exactly when surgical intervention became beneficial.

Table 4.1 shows the proportion of the reduction of mortality which occurred after the introduction of specific measures: about a quarter (0·25) of the fall from all airborne diseases and (as shown in the last column) about a tenth of that from all diseases (infective and non-infective).

The reduction of the death-rate attributable to immunization and therapy was of course much less than these figures suggest. Mortality from all the diseases was declining before, and in most cases long before, effective procedures became available. It is doubtful whether a reliable estimate can be made of the effect of medical measures on the whole class of airborne diseases, but it is probably safe to conclude that they were not the main influence on the trend of mortality even from the time when immunization or treatment became available, except in the case of tuberculosis and, less certainly, diphtheria. Their contribution will be examined further in Chapter 6.

WATER- AND FOOD-BORNE DISEASES (see Table 3.4)

Cholera, diarrhoea, and dysentery. In the mid nineteenth century cholera was grouped with other diarrhoeal diseases in the Registrar-General's classification; however the last epidemic in Britain was in 1865, and from that time the contribution of cholera was negligible. Mortality from the diarrhoeal diseases fell in the late nineteenth century; it increased between 1901 and 1911 but decreased rapidly from that time.

It is unlikely that treatment had any appreciable effect on the outcome of the diseases before the use of intravenous therapy in the 1930s; by which time 95 per cent of the improvement had occurred. For the main explanation of the fall of mortality we must look to the hygienic measures which reduced exposure.

Non-respiratory tuberculosis. Non-respiratory tuberculosis was an important cause of death in the nineteenth century. Although mortality fell quite rapidly after 1901, there was still a considerable number of deaths in England and Wales (197) in 1971.

Interpretation is complicated by the fact that non-respiratory tuberculosis is due to both human and bovine infections; the abdominal cases are predominantly bovine, whereas those involving bones and other organs are often caused by the human organism. The human types can be interpreted in the same terms as the pulmonary disease, but a different explanation must be sought for the bovine infection. It is unlikely that treatment contributed significantly to the fall of mortality, since the level was already low when streptomycin, the first effective measure, was introduced in 1947.

Typhoid and typhus. As noted in Chapter 3, mortality from typhus fell rapidly in the late nineteenth century and there have been few deaths in the twentieth. It can be said without hesitation that specific medical measures had no influence on this reduction.

The decline of enteric fevers was also rapid, and began before the turn of the century, somewhat earlier than the decrease of deaths from diarrhoea and dysentery. Effective treatment by chloramphenicol was not available until 1950, but by that time mortality from enteric fever was almost eliminated from England and Wales. Although immunization was used widely in the armed services during the war, its effectiveness is doubtful and it can have had little influence on the number of deaths.

In summary, the rapid decline of mortality from diseases spread by water and food since the late nineteenth century owed little to medical intervention. Immunization is relatively ineffective even today, and therapeutic measures of some value were not employed until about 1950, by which time the number of deaths had fallen to a low level.

OTHER DISEASES DUE TO MICRO-ORGANISMS (see Table 3.5)
Convulsions and teething. As mentioned previously, most of the deaths included under these unsatisfactory terms were due to infectious diseases of childhood, for example to whooping cough, measles, otitis media, meningitis, and gastro-enteritis. These infections are mainly airborne, and the general conclusions concerning the airborne diseases may be accepted for them. That is to say, it is unlikely that immunization and therapy had any significant effect on the frequency of death before the introduction of sulphonamides and antibiotics, and even after that time they were probably less important than other influences.

Syphilis. Although syphilis was associated with only 0·3 per cent of the reduction of mortality from the mid nineteenth century to 1971, it remained an important cause of sickness and death until about 1916, when salvarsan was made available without charge to medical practitioners. From this time the number of deaths fell, and was quite low in 1945 when penicillin largely replaced the arsenical preparations.

The decline of syphilis since its introduction to Europe in the fifteenth century was not due mainly to therapy, for after several centuries the disease had changed to a milder form. Nevertheless it seems right to attribute the fall of mortality since 1901 essentially to treatment. It should of course be recognized that effective treatment, as in the case of tuberculosis, not only benefits those affected by the disease, but also reduces the number of persons who spread the infection. It seems justified to regard this secondary effect as a further contribution of treatment.

Appendicitis, peritonitis. Mortality from these causes increased slightly during the nineteenth and early twentieth centuries, probably because of more accurate certification of cause of death, but declined after 1921. This improvement, which accounted for 0·4 per cent of the fall of the death-rate from all causes, can be attributed to treatment.

Puerperal fever. The death-rate from puerperal fever declined from the beginning of this century, but more rapidly after the introduction of the sulphonamides (1935) and, later, penicillin. It seems probable that the initial fall was due mainly to reduced exposure to infection during labour; but from 1935 the obstetric services were greatly strengthened by chemotherapy. Both influences can be credited to medical measures.

Other infections. The other conditions shown in Table 3.5 are a miscellaneous group, including some well recognized diseases which caused few deaths, either because they were uncommon in this period (as in the case of malaria, tetanus, poliomyelitis, and encephalitis) or because although common they were not often lethal (in the case of mumps, chicken pox, and rubella). They also include some relatively infrequent certified causes of death which are ill-defined, such as abscess, phlegmon, and pyaemia. In addition there is a very small number of deaths due to worm parasites which, strictly, do not belong among conditions due to microorganisms.

These infections were associated with 3·5 per cent of the fall of mortality between the mid nineteenth century and 1971. In view of their varied aetiology it is not possible to assess accurately the major influences, but it is unlikely that therapy made much contribution before 1935. More than half of the reduction of deaths occurred before this time.

The conclusions concerning the contribution of immunization and therapy to the decline of the infections may be summarized as follows. Except in the case of vaccination against smallpox (which was associated with 1·6 per cent of the decline of the death-rate from 1848–54 to 1971), it is unlikely that immunization or therapy had a significant effect on mortality from infectious diseases before the twentieth century. Between 1900 and 1935 these measures contributed in some diseases: antitoxin in treatment of diphtheria; surgery in treatment of appendicitis, peritonitis, and ear infections; salvarsan in treatment of syphilis; intravenous therapy in treatment of diarrhoeal diseases; passive immunization against tetanus; and improved obstetric care resulting in prevention of puerperal fever. But even if these measures were responsible for the whole decline of mortality from these conditions after 1900, which clearly they were not, they would account for only a small part of the decrease of deaths which occurred before 1935. From that time the first powerful chemotherapeutic agents, sulphonamides and, later, antibiotics, came into use, and they were supplemented by improved vaccines. However, they were certainly not the only influences which led to the continued fall of mortality. I conclude that immunization and treatment contributed little to the reduction of deaths from infectious diseases before 1935, and over the whole period since cause of death was first registered (in 1838) they were much less important than other influences. In the light of the conclusions concerning the twentieth century, it is most unlikely that medical measures had a significant effect on the trend of mortality in the eighteenth and early nineteenth centuries.

REDUCTION OF EXPOSURE TO INFECTION

Clearly, at least part of the decline of mortality from infectious diseases was due to reduced contact with micro-organisms. In developed countries an individual no longer meets the cholera vibrio, he is rarely exposed to the typhoid organism and he is infected by the tubercle bacillus much less often than in the past. But so far as can be judged there has been no considerable change in frequency of exposure to the streptococcus or the measles virus, and we must look elsewhere for an explanation of the decline of deaths from scarlet fever and measles.

The possibility of control of transmission of micro-organisms is determined largely by the ways they are spread. It is relatively easy (in developed countries) to prevent exposure to water-borne diseases; it is more difficult to control those spread by food, personal contact, and animal vectors; and it is usually impossible to prevent transmission of airborne infections.

AIRBORNE DISEASES

Since it is not possible to prevent transmission of airborne infections, it would seem to follow that reduction of exposure to them has played little part in the fall of mortality. However, this conclusion needs some qualification.

Although it is very difficult to prevent transmission of airborne diseases from one individual to another, less frequent exposure has nevertheless contributed to the decline of mortality from some infections. There are broadly two ways in which this has come about. The first is as a result of a reduction of prevalence; smallpox, syphilis, and tuberculosis are much less common than in the past, and exposure to them is correspondingly reduced. The second way is by improved living and working conditions, which prevent contact with infectious people in the community. However, these influences are not effective with all airborne diseases. In the case of a highly infectious condition such as measles, in communities in which it is endemic nearly all children became infected, in spite of improvements in living conditions and a large reduction in the number of serious cases.

In several of the airborne infections associated with the decline of mortality (Table 3.3) prevention of exposure has contributed little if anything to the decrease in the number of deaths. Although the death-rate from measles has fallen to a low level, infection rates remain high. There is no effective control of the organisms which cause bronchitis and pneumonia, and the influences which determine the disappearance and reappearance of the influenza virus are not well understood. The streptococcus, which is responsible for scarlet fever and for most of the infections of the ear, pharynx, and larynx, is ubiquitous, and the decline of these conditions owes little to reduced contact. However, in the case of the other diseases shown in Table 3.3 (tuberculosis, whooping cough, diphtheria, and smallpox) exposure to infection is undoubtedly less common than in the past. The change has come about, not as a primary influence, but as a secondary effect of other causes which reduced the prevalence of the diseases in the community. With the exception of smallpox and, possibly, tuberculosis, this influence was probably delayed until the twentieth century.

WATER- AND FOOD-BORNE DISEASES

It is in this class of diseases that a substantial reduction of mortality is likely to be achieved by prevention of exposure. The water- and food-borne diseases associated with the decline of the death-rate since the mid nineteenth century in England and Wales are shown in Table 3.4. The table also includes typhus which is vector-borne, but cannot be separated from typhoid in national statistics before 1871.

The death-rate from these diseases fell continuously from the second half of the nineteenth century. (The exception is gastro-enteritis of infancy, whose decline was delayed until the twentieth century.) There is no doubt that the fall of mortality from these diseases was due to reduced exposure brought about by improvements in hygiene: their spread is due to defective sanitary arrangements, and their decline coincided with the advances in the nineteenth century, particularly in purification of water and sewage disposal. The trend owed nothing to immunization or therapy, and little, if anything, to a change in the character of the diseases.

For many years the decline of gastro-enteritis presented a problem (a central one in the interpretation of infant mortality) which arose from uncertainty about the infective nature of the disease. It is now clear that the provision of a safe milk supply was the main reason for the reduction of deaths from gastro-enteritis and contributed substantially to the fall of infant mortality from 1900.

The other water- and food-borne disease which contributed substantially to the reduction of mortality was non-respiratory tuberculosis. The death-rate from the disease declined from 1848–54; considerably in the second half of the nineteenth century and even more rapidly after 1900. Although deaths due to human and bovine infections cannot be separated in national statistics, it seems probable that the human types were associated with the decline before 1900 and both types after 1900. In this case the fall of mortality in the nineteenth century can be discussed in the same terms as that of respiratory tuberculosis: it was not due to medical measures, or to a change in the character of the disease. The abdominal cases, however, were caused largely by infected milk, and their decline can be attributed to elimination of tuberculous cattle and to the more general measures taken to protect milk supplies after 1900.

OTHER DISEASES DUE TO MICRO-ORGANISMS

Most of the deaths shown under this heading were classified unsatisfactorily under convulsions and teething; several of them were undoubtedly due to airborne infections and their decline probably owed little to reduction of exposure. The infections (in Table 3.5) which were affected were syphilis and puerperal fever, whose contributions to the fall of mortality were, however, very small. Moreover in the case of syphilis the less frequent exposure was a secondary result of treatment of the disease which decreased the number of infective persons, rather than a primary influence. In puerperal fever, exposure to infection was reduced by improved midwifery practice, following the teaching of Semmelweis.

Since reliable information about the diseases which declined in the eighteenth and early nineteenth centuries is not available, the possibility that exposure to infection was reduced at that time can only be assessed in general terms. Population growth and industrialization created optimum conditions for the propagation and spread of airborne infections, and if any reduction of exposure occurred it could have come about only as a secondary consequence of other influences which diminished the prevalence of the diseases in the community. It is, however, in respect of the water- and food-borne diseases that the question of exposure is most important.

It is upon purification of water, efficient disposal of sewage and food hygiene that reduction of exposure to water- and food-borne diseases primarily depends. There are grounds for thinking that at least the first two of these influences deteriorated in the early nineteenth century when, under the pressure of population growth, the primitive sewage systems deteriorated, and drinking water became more heavily polluted. It was not until the second half of the nineteenth century that these risks were largely controlled.

One can be less confident about the trend of food hygiene in the same period. What is clear is that there was little if any improvement in respect of milk, the most important component of the diet as a vehicle for transmission of disease. In an examination of the relation between milk supplies, infant mortality, and population growth, Beaver concluded that although the quantity of milk increased from the eighteenth century, it must have been heavily contaminated by pathogens.[1] It was not until the late nineteenth century that commercial pasteurization and bottling of milk were introduced, and not until the twentieth century that a safe supply became generally available.

Since most solid foods are protected, not by sterilization and sealing as in the case of milk, but by precautions in handling and distribution involving many people, it is not possible to say when the transition from an infected to a safe supply was achieved. However, it seems unlikely that food hygiene improved in the pre-registration period; indeed, it probably deteriorated, since the growth of towns made it necessary to transport large quantities of food from rural to urban areas, and thus resulted in increased handling and delayed consumption. A substantial advance in food hygiene was delayed until the present century, and rested largely on the work of microbiologists in the preceding fifty years.

Improvement in personal hygiene also can have little influence on the trend of mortality, except possibly in the case of typhus. Unwashed bodies and infrequently changed clothing and bedding provide ideal conditions for the body lice which carry the organism, and the low standards of cleanliness which prevailed before the nineteenth century no doubt contributed, perhaps substantially, to the prevalence of the disease. Standards began to improve in the late eighteenth century, first among the well-to-do, but later in all classes, and this change may have had some effect on the fall of mortality. However the epidemiology of the disease is complex, and it is unlikely that any single influence accounted for its decline and eventual disappearance.

IMPROVEMENT IN NUTRITION

If the decline of mortality from infectious diseases was not due to a change in the character of the diseases, and owed little to reduced exposure to micro-organisms before the second half of the nineteenth century or to immunization and therapy before the

1. Beaver, M. W., 'Population, infant mortality and milk', *Population Studies*, 27 (1973), 243.

twentieth, the possibility which remains is that the response to infections was modified by an advance in man's health brought about by improved nutrition.

There are two grounds for believing that the improvement in health which occurred before the late nineteenth century was due essentially to better nutrition: (*a*) there was a large increase in home-grown food, enough to feed a population which trebled between 1700 and 1850 without significant food imports; and (*b*) in the conditions which existed at that time, an advance in nutrition was a necessary condition for a substantial and prolonged reduction of mortality.

THE INCREASE IN FOOD SUPPLIES

Estimates of food production were unreliable before the first agricultural census of Britain in 1865, and it was not until 1884 that national statistics of production and yield became available. The evidence that food production increased in the eighteenth and early nineteenth centuries is therefore of two kinds: circumstantial, from estimates of land areas under cultivation, yields per acre and amounts of imported and exported food; and inferential, from the fact that a greatly expanded population was fed on home-grown food.

For what they are worth, estimates of grain and meat production in the eighteenth century suggest that it at least kept pace with the increasing population; in some years there was a small surplus of grain for export. However during the last years of the century there was a succession of poor harvests, which led to widespread food shortages and forced the government to lift the ban on importing of animal products from Ireland and to prohibit exporting of grain. These difficulties were temporary, and during the first half of the nineteenth century both the amount of land devoted to cereal production and the yield per acre continued to increase. In 1840, the quantity of imported wheat relative to total consumption was no more than it had been in 1811 (about 5 per cent); but the population of Britain had increased during the period by 6·5 million (55 per cent). After 1885, imports of wheat, especially from North America, rose substantially and this permitted some reduction in the area of land used for wheat production in Britain. Imports of other foods also increased, and by 1870 about a fifth of the nation's food came from abroad.

Not much reliance can be placed on estimates of food production during the eighteenth and early nineteenth centuries. Evidence which is more convincing is that the greatly expanded population was fed on home-grown food. The population of England and Wales increased from an estimated 5·5 million in 1702 to 8·9 in 1801 and 17·9 in 1851. Since exports and imports of food during this period were relatively small, it is clear that food production must have at least trebled to sustain an increase of 12·4 million in a century and a half.

Whether the population was better fed in the eighteenth and nineteenth centuries is another question. Certainly there were no direct observations on the nutrition of individuals which would enable us to draw this conclusion; and from the conflicting views of economic historians about the trend of food production per head, it is clear that this type of evidence is not decisive. I shall therefore approach the question by examining the relation between malnutrition and infectious disease.

MALNUTRITION AND INFECTIOUS DISEASE

It is well recognized that the health of an individual has a profound bearing on his reaction to infectious disease. Measles is an example of a condition in which infection rates are high in all social classes, but the likelihood of serious illness and death depends largely on the health of the child and is much increased among the poor. It is also clear that the general state of health is determined by multiple influences, including particularly previous illnesses and nutrition.

It is more difficult to go beyond these generalizations to a precise estimate of the part played by nutrition in determining the outcome of infectious disease. There are many conflicting reports in the literature, and disorders of metabolism and deficiency diseases were accorded a relatively minor role in the health of man and animals until recently. However Newberne and Williams have reviewed experimental evidence of nutritional influences on infections.[1] They suggested that the effect of an infection depends

1. Newberne, P. M., and Williams, G., 'Nutritional influence on the course of infections', in Dunlop, R. H., and Moon, H. W. (eds), *Resistance to Infectious Disease* (Saskatoon Modern Press, 1970), p. 93.

63

to a considerable degree on the nutritional condition of an animal at the time of exposure. A severe degree of deficiency of almost any of the essential nutrients may have a marked effect on the manner in which the host responds to an infectious agent. The same infection may be mild or even inapparent in a well-nourished animal, but virulent and sometimes fatal in one that is mal-nourished. They refer to four ways in which nutrition influences infection:

(1) effects on the host which facilitate initial invasion of the infectious agent; (2) through an effect on the agent once it is established in the tissues; (3) through an effect on secondary infection; or (4) by retarding convalescence after infec-tion.

They concluded that

Grossly inadequate intakes of protein and other specific nutrients are today re-sulting in extreme degrees of malnutrition and concomitant infectious disease. It seems likely that the interaction between nutrition and infection are more important in animal and human populations than one would predict from the results of laboratory investigations. It must be remembered that the interaction between nutrition and infection is dynamic, being frequently characterized by synergism and less commonly by antagonism, and that control of malnutrition and infection are interdependent, so that the course of a disease is intimately related to the nutritional status of the host.

In man also it has proved difficult to obtain unequivocal results, for as food shortage and other features of poverty usually occur together, their respective contributions to mortality are hard to separate. For example, populations in which tuberculosis, or in a tropical country, schistosomiasis, are common are likely to be poor, underfed, and exposed to infection; and it is not easy to determine the relative importance of malnutrition and frequent exposure. There is some evidence of a quasi-experimental kind in the increased incidence of infectious diseases in populations whose food intake was reduced substantially during the two world wars.

However, knowledge of the relation between malnutrition and infection has been extended considerably in recent years through experience of the World Health Organization in developing countries, where infectious diseases are still predominant. This leaves no doubt that malnutrition contributes largely to the high level of infectious deaths; the populations are more prone to infections and suffer more seriously when they are infected. Moreover, infectious diseases have an unfavourable effect on nutritional state, and the interaction between disease and malnutrition leads to a vicious cycle which is characteristic of poverty and underdevelopment. These effects are not restricted to respiratory and intestinal infections for which there are no specific vaccines; mortality remains high from measles and whooping cough for which effective immunization is available, and indeed it is questionable whether infectious diseases can be controlled by vaccination in a malnourished population. The problems are particularly serious in infancy, before the child has developed its own natural defence mechanisms. The World Health Organization concluded that 'one half to three quarters of all statistically recorded deaths of infants and young children are attributed to a combination of malnutrition and infection'.[1] The deficiency is due mainly to lack of calories and proteins, although mineral and vitamin deficiencies are frequently associated.

It should be emphasized that the malnutrition which is the common background of infectious diseases in developing countries is not necessarily, and is not usually of the overt types such as rickets, beri-beri, pellagra, and the protein-calorie deficiency syndromes, kwashiorkor and marasmus; it is more often manifested as chronic malnutrition without specific features which are easily recognized. Two-thirds of the populations of some countries are estimated to suffer from this less obvious kind of deficiency, in which infection is frequently the final influence which results in death. The interpretation of this experience was discussed in a recent report from the World Health Organization.

A debilitated organism is far less resistant to attacks by invading micro-organisms. Ordinary measles or diarrhoea—harmless and short-lived diseases among well fed children—are usually serious and often fatal to the chronically malnourished. Before vaccines existed, practically every child in all countries caught measles, but 300 times more deaths occurred in the poorer countries than in the richer ones. The reason was not that the virus was more virulent, nor that there were fewer medical services; but that in poorly nourished communities the microbes attack a host which, because of chronic malnutrition, is less able to resist. The same happens with diarrhoea, respiratory infections,

1. World Health Organization, *Better Food for a Healthier World*, Features, FS/19 (1973).

tuberculosis and many other common infections to which malnourished populations pay a heavy and unnecessary toll.[1]

The same report gave the results of a recent investigation of mortality in infancy in Latin America, which concluded that 'when malnutrition was not given as the major cause of death in official statistics, it was an associated cause in 50–80 per cent of cases. Malnutrition was also a concomitant factor in 60 per cent of the deaths attributable to measles'. The author concluded that malnutrition was the most serious health problem among the populations studied.

These and other investigations show the enormous importance of nutrition in determining the outcome of infection, and the tragic synergistic relation which exists between malnutrition and infectious disease. The World Health Organization report suggested that 'we have given too much attention to the enemy and have to some extent overlooked our own defences'. That is to say we have concentrated on specific measures such as vaccination and environmental improvement without sufficient regard for the predominant part played by nutritional state. 'For the time being,' it concluded, 'an adequate diet is the most effective "vaccine" against most of the diarrhoeal, respiratory and other common infections.'

INFECTIOUS DISEASES AFTER THE FIRST AGRICULTURAL REVOLUTION

It is against the background of this understanding of the relation between malnutrition and infectious disease that experience of the infections must be interpreted. The conclusion that the reduction of mortality and the beginning of the modern rise of population resulted from an increase in food supplies rests largely on the belief that the size of human populations had been limited previously by lack of food, and that an increase was a necessary condition for a substantial and prolonged expansion. I must now examine the grounds for this conclusion.

Until about 10,000 years ago, the main restraint on population growth was a high level of mortality determined directly or

1. Behar, M., 'A deadly combination', *World Health* (February-March, 1974), p. 29.

indirectly by lack of food. The increase in food supplies which resulted from the first agricultural revolution lowered mortality and led to an expansion of numbers, an expansion which continued to the point at which food resources became again marginal. The aggregation of populations of substantial size created the conditions required for the propagation and transmission of micro-organisms, particularly those that are airborne. Many organisms did not survive contact with man; others achieved a relationship which was unharmful and, occasionally, mutually beneficial; a minority caused sickness and death of their hosts. However, the effects of this minority of micro-organisms on human health were so devastating that infectious diseases became the predominant cause of death, something they had not been during man's evolution and are not today for other animals living in their natural habitats.

But although this may describe the circumstances under which infectious diseases became predominant, it does not account for the significance of malnutrition; indeed at first sight it would appear to be an advantage for a parasite to have a well-fed host, and surprising that an improvement in human nutrition since the eighteenth century should have been a disaster for certain micro-organisms.

For most micro-organisms it is probably desirable to have a well-nourished host, and no disadvantages have resulted to them from the better nutrition of the past few centuries. But the relationship between man and organisms which cause disease is unstable, and finely balanced according to the physiological state of host and parasite. It was critical to this relationship that it evolved over a period when the human host was, in general, poorly nourished, because numbers had expanded beyond the point at which they could be maintained in health by the available food resources. It is therefore understandable that an improvement in human health, brought about by an advance in nutrition, should have tipped the balance of advantage in favour of the host and against the parasite. Hence the better nutrition was a necessary condition for a substantial and prolonged decline of mortality; without it immunization and therapy would have been of little value and reduction of exposure to some organisms less effective.

This theoretical appraisal of the relation between malnutrition and infection is in keeping with extensive recent experience in developing countries, described above.

It is unfortunate that the infections which declined cannot be identified reliably before 1838. They no doubt included typhus and smallpox, but it is unlikely that these diseases were sufficiently common to account for a substantial proportion of the total reduction of mortality. In the years after registration tuberculosis was the predominant cause of death, and since the death-rate from the disease was declining rapidly from the time of registration, it seems probable that it was doing so at least in the years immediately before. Whether tuberculosis had the same importance in the eighteenth century is an open question.

However, present-day experience in developing countries again suggests what may be offered, with reservations, as a possible answer. There is little doubt that the reduction of mortality in the eighteenth and early nineteenth centuries occurred predominantly in childhood. Improvement in nutrition would have lowered the number of deaths from all or nearly all the common infections, including the respiratory and, particularly, the diarrhoeal diseases. Indeed the investigations in Latin America referred to above suggest that the diarrhoeal diseases, which accounted for most of the deaths in childhood, are likely to have been those chiefly affected.

This interpretation is consistent with evidence from national statistics for England and Wales (after 1838) although it leaves open the question of the relative importance of tuberculosis before and after registration. It is also uncertain whether the improvement in childhood mortality affected children in the first year of life. The fact that infant mortality was 150 (per 1,000 live-births) when first recorded in 1838, suggests that the rate may have fallen earlier; and Beaver suggested that 'a reduction in this rate was associated with agricultural and commercial developments during the second half of the eighteenth century, whereby cow's milk was made generally available both in town and country throughout the year'.[1] He also concluded that 'a further reduction in infant

1. Beaver, M. W., 'Population, infant mortality and milk', *Population Studies,* **27** (1973), 243.

mortality took place at the beginning of this century; this was associated with commercial developments within the dairy industry which favour a pathogen-free milk'. That is to say the first major advance in infancy resulted from an increase in the amount of milk, and the second from an improvement in its safety.

This conclusion in respect of the first year of life is broadly in accord with the interpretation suggested for the decline of mortality at later ages (predominantly in childhood). The death-rate fell in the eighteenth and nineteenth centuries because of an increase in food supplies which led to better nutrition. From the second half of the nineteenth century this advance was strongly supported by reduction of exposure to infection which resulted indirectly from the falling prevalence of disease, and directly from improved hygiene affecting, in the first instance, the quality of water and food. With the exception of vaccination against smallpox (whose contribution to the total decline of mortality was small), the impact of medical procedures of immunization and therapy was delayed until the twentieth century.

5

Non-infective conditions

The evidence for England and Wales suggests that with the possible exceptions of infanticide and starvation, about which information is lacking, non-infective causes of death were not associated with the decline of mortality before 1900. In the twentieth century, however, the reduction of deaths from non-infective conditions was considerable; moreover it has been concealed to some extent by the increase in mortality from lung cancer and myocardial infarction, brought about by smoking and other influences. In this brief examination of reasons for the decline of non-infective deaths the effect of these increases will be ignored (it would be very difficult to take account of them) and the causes of death associated with the decline will be referred to in order according to their contribution to the reduction of mortality.

DEATHS IN THE TWENTIETH CENTURY

Much the largest fall (1,057 deaths per million between 1901 and 1971) was associated with the heterogeneous class, 'prematurity, immaturity and other diseases of infancy' (Table 3.6). These deaths were almost restricted to the first year of life, and their contribution to the decline of infant mortality was of the same order of magnitude as that of deaths due to an infection: gastro-enteritis. In 1901 more than 90 per cent of them were certified under two headings, 'premature birth' and 'atrophy, debility'. The latter no longer appears in the Registrar-General's classification, so that the large decrease in the number of deaths is explained by transfers to other causes, many of which have of course declined. Premature birth had no consistent meaning in 1901; it was later identified with low birth-weight until the internationally agreed basis was changed, to take account of the duration of

70

gestation. With due regard for these inconsistencies, there has undoubtedly been a large reduction in deaths of this type in the first year of life. This contribution to the fall of the non-infective death-rate was probably due in part to a rising standard of living, particularly improvement in maternal nutrition which lowered the incidence of premature birth, and in part to improved obstetric care (before and during labour) and better management of the premature infant.

Nothing more need be said about deaths attributed to 'old age' in 1901, whose rapid decline was evidently due to transfers to more satisfactory diagnoses. Next in magnitude (according to their contribution to the fall of the death-rate in the twentieth century) were 'other diseases', which comprised a considerable number of causes of death, many of which would today be unacceptable. The largest reductions were associated with alcoholism, rickets, and non-infective diseases of the respiratory system other than emphysema and asthma, and are probably explained in part by less frequent drinking, improved nutrition, and, particularly in the case of the respiratory diseases, better certification. There were also some causes of death (for example, eczema) whose decline was no doubt largely due to treatment.

'Other diseases of digestive system' exclude cancers, but include some causes of death whose decrease was due to better certification (for example, gastric catarrh). The largest reductions appear to have been associated with conditions now treated by surgery (gall bladder disease, hernia, and intestinal obstruction) and with cirrhosis whose decline is attributable to less frequent drinking.

The next two classes, rheumatic heart disease and nephritis, are essentially infective and are misplaced in this discussion. They have been included only because Table 3.6 examined the trend of mortality in the nineteenth as well as the twentieth century, and for 1848–54 these infections cannot be separated from non-infective causes of death. To this extent the estimate of the contribution of non-infective conditions to the fall of the death-rate is overstated.

There seems little doubt that the decline of mortality from violence in the twentieth century, when the frequency of accidents has risen steadily, was due predominantly to surgery.

71

The deaths under 'other diseases of nervous system' include brain tumour, diseases of the cord and neuritis, where the diagnoses must be in doubt. The improvement was mainly in respect of epilepsy, and may be attributed to treatment. The reasons for the reduction of the death-rate from cerebrovascular disease is not clear, and the contributions of the two remaining classes (other diseases of urinary system and pregnancy and childbirth, excluding sepsis) were small.

From this brief analysis it is evident that interpretation of the trend of non-infective causes of death can be attempted only in very general terms; the influences are more varied and less specific than in the case of the infections. Therapeutic measures made a substantial contribution in respect of some causes of death; for example there is little doubt about the value of surgery in cases of violence and in several digestive disorders. It is not possible to be equally confident about the effects of treatment on some other conditions listed in Table 3.6. The heterogeneous class of deaths ascribed to prematurity, immaturity, other diseases of infancy made the largest contribution to the total decline of mortality. These deaths were almost restricted to the first year of life, and their reduction, together with that of deaths due to gastro-enteritis, was the main reason for the rapid fall of infant mortality from the beginning of the century. While this trend no doubt owed something to improvements in obstetric services, before and during labour, it was probably due mainly to advances in maternal nutrition and better infant feeding and care. Some of the decline shown in Table 3.6 was associated with changes in classification of causes of death, and in two cases at least (rheumatic fever and nephritis) was due to inclusion of what were essentially infective causes of death.

DEATHS BEFORE THE TWENTIETH CENTURY

INFANTICIDE

I referred above to Langer's review of the history of infanticide, which suggested that it was practised on a substantial scale, at least until the second half of the nineteenth century, and probably in some developing countries until the present day.[1] Although this conclusion cannot be confirmed by national statistics, for obvious reasons, it is nevertheless consistent with extensive historical evidence assembled by Langer and others. That infanticide remained common at least until the late nineteenth century is suggested by the fact that Stevenson and his family were surprised to find that there were few children in the populations they encountered on the islands in the Pacific.

But although infanticide was probably common in the eighteenth and previous centuries, it is not possible to say exactly when the practice declined. It seems likely that it became less frequent as the growth of foundling hospitals made it possible for a mother to get rid of an unwanted child rather than destroy it. This development is well illustrated by the experience of a foundling hospital in St Petersburg, described by Langer:

By the mid 1830s it had 25,000 children on its rolls and was admitting 5000 newcomers annually. Since no questions were asked and the place was attractive, almost half of the new-born babies were deposited there by their parents. A dozen doctors and 600 wet-nurses were in attendance to care for the children during the first six weeks, after which they were sent to peasant nurses in the country. At the age of six (if they survived to that age) they were returned to St Petersburg for systematic education. The programme was excellent, but its aims were impossible to achieve. Despite all excellent management and professional efforts, thirty to forty per cent of the children died during the first six weeks and hardly a third reached the age of six.

In England, Parliament (1756) made provision for asylums for exposed or deserted young children to be opened in all countries, ridings, and divisions of the kingdom; and in France, Napoleon in 1811 decreed that there should be hospitals in every department. However the demand was far beyond the resources of the foundling institutions, and it was not until the last quarter of the nineteenth century that the practice of infanticide became uncommon and not until the twentieth that (in western Europe) it virtually disappeared. Its decline occurred over approximately the same period as the fall of the birth-rate, and while many other developments may have contributed (for example improved living conditions and maternal and child welfare services) the main influence

1. Langer, W. L., 'Infanticide: a historical survey', *History of Childhood Quarterly*, I (1974), 353.

was undoubtedly the growth of contraceptive practices which reduced the number of unwanted births.

STARVATION

This is another non-infective cause of death which may have declined significantly in the pre-registration period and later. Again, statistical evidence is deficient. Moreover, as noted in the preceding chapter, unless food supplies are very inadequate, there are many more cases of chronic malnutrition associated with infectious diseases but without definitive signs, than there are cases with specific evidence (such as rickets or kwashiorkor) of deficiency or frank starvation. But if it is accepted that the nutrition of the population was poor at the beginning of the eighteenth century and has improved continuously since that time, it seems likely that some people must have been at or near starvation level and that their number decreased. This conclusion is not difficult to accept for the eighteenth and nineteenth centuries, when it is recognized that in the wealthiest countries there are sections of the population who are underfed even in the present day.

I conclude that the decline of mortality from non-infective causes of death (infanticide and starvation in the eighteenth and nineteenth centuries and a large number of conditions in the twentieth) was due partly to medical measures, but also to contraception and improvement in nutrition. Indeed, since the reduction of deaths from infanticide probably made the largest contribution to the decline, the change in reproductive behaviour which resulted in avoidance of unwanted pregnancies may have been the most important influence on the decrease of deaths from non-infective conditions.

6

Behaviour, environment, and therapy

The preceding chapters were concerned with the modern improvement in health, as indicated by the reduction of deaths from infective and non-infective causes during the past three centuries. The present chapter examines, in the light of the conclusions, the nature of the influences (behavioural, environmental, and therapeutic) that have been at work; it also considers whether the relative importance of the different influences has been modified by the change in the character of health problems which followed the decline of the infections.

INFLUENCES ON HEALTH IN THE PAST

The review of diseases which declined (Chapter 3) suggested that if we put aside deaths due to infanticide and starvation and to certain non-infective causes which have decreased in the twentieth century, interpretation of the modern transformation of health requires essentially an explanation for the decline of the infections. We must therefore consider more closely the major influences referred to in Chapter 4.

NUTRITION

It was suggested that an improvement in nutrition was the critical advance which led to the modern reduction of mortality and growth of population. For about the first half of the time from the early eighteenth century to the present day, it was unsupported by other measures; and over the whole period it has been more effective than environmental, therapeutic, and behavioural influences. The following are the grounds on which this conclusion rests.

1. It is necessary first to make what may seem an obvious point: that something remarkable has happened since the seventeenth

century. Some biologists have arrived at a rather different conclusion: recognizing the changing character of infectious diseases, and the difficulty of assessing the multiple influences (genetic, therapeutic, environmental, and nutritional) which affect their behaviour, they have attributed the decline of the infections, individually and in some cases collectively, to what Greenwood referred to as the 'ever-varying state of the immunological constitution of the herd'.[1] To accept this interpretation, however, we should have to believe either: (*a*) that a reduction of mortality from most of the common diseases occurred fortuitously, unaffected by the agricultural and industrial developments of the past three centuries; or (*b*) that one or more adverse influences in this period led to high mortality, which by natural selection rsulted in populations more resistant to infectious disease. On the second assumption, the modern advance in health was due to poor living conditions rather than to improvements, and populations would be more resistant to micro-organisms today than in the past (whereas with diminished exposure it is probable that they are, if anything, genetically less resistant). It would also seem to follow that the correct approach to the health problems of developing countries, where infectious diseases are still predominant, would be either to wait patiently for a fortuitous reduction of mortality, or to permit conditions to deteriorate further, in the expectation that in time natural selection, operating through high mortality, would lead to the birth of healthier populations.

2. A second consideration which bears upon the nutritional hypothesis is that the alternative explanations which can be suggested are clearly inadequate. They are discussed below; but briefly, it seems inconceivable that in the early years of industrialization there were improvements in environmental conditions which led to reduction of exposure to infectious diseases, or that medical measures had an influence on health in the eighteenth and nineteenth centuries which they have not had in the twentieth.

3. There was a large increase in food supplies from about the end of the seventeenth century. Although this cannot be demonstrated

---

1. Greenwood, M., 'English death rates past, present and future', *Journal of the Royal Statistical Society*, **99** (1936).

convincingly from the deficient statistics for the period, it seems a reasonable deduction from the fact that the population of England and Wales trebled between 1700 and 1850 when there were no substantial food imports.

4. The fourth line of evidence is the one I find most persuasive: that in the conditions which existed before the eighteenth century an improvement in nutrition was a necessary condition for a substantial and sustained decline of mortality and growth of population. The ideas on which this conclusion is based are as follows.

(*a*) For early man, as for animals in their natural habitats, numbers born were considerably greater than the environment could support (or, stated differently, fertility was not restricted with regard for the resources of the environment).

(*b*) Numbers of early men and other animals were limited by a high level of mortality attributable directly or indirectly to lack of food. Direct deaths were those from starvation and associated disease, indirect mainly from homicide or predation determined also by the resources of the environment, particularly its food supplies.

(*c*) Disease, and particularly infectious disease, was not a serious problem for early man, as it is not for wild animals. Rigorous selection (the large majority of those born alive died or were killed before they could reproduce) kept the frequency of disease and disability at a low level; and at a low density of a few persons per square mile, human populations in frequent contact were not large enough to permit the propagation and transmission of most micro-organisms, particularly the airborne.

(*d*) The first agricultural revolution led to the aggregation of populations and produced the food needed to sustain them. However in the absence of effective birth control numbers expanded to the level where food supplies became again marginal.

(*e*) The large populations created the conditions needed for survival of the common infections and led to a high level of mortality from infectious disease. The relation between man and the organisms which cause disease was thus established in malnourished populations. In these circumstances an advance in nutrition was a necessary condition for the decline of the infections and improvement in health.

77

(*f*) An advance in nutrition required an increase in food supplies and restraint of population growth if it was to be maintained. These conditions were met in the eighteenth and nineteenth centuries, by increased agricultural production from the end of the seventeenth century, and by falling birth-rates from the nineteenth.

(*g*) Finally, I believe that this interpretation is in accord with experience of developing countries today, outlined in Chapter 4.

Before ending this discussion of nutrition I should consider briefly an objection which has been raised to the conclusion: that there was a substantial increase in life-expectation of the aristocracy during the eighteenth and nineteenth centuries, although it is unlikely that well-to-do people offered much scope for improvement in nutrition. If we can accept that their expectation of life did increase, and one hesitates to rely on statistical data for the period before births and deaths were recorded nationally, two possible explanations can be considered.

One is that in the eighteenth and nineteenth centuries, when the prevalence of infectious disease was declining in the general population, all sections benefited from the secondary effects of reduced exposure. This possibility is well illustrated by experience of tuberculosis in the past century. The disease occurred in wealthy people, although less often and less seriously than among the poor. The difference between the social classes was determined partly by different levels of exposure, but also by the better nutrition of the well-to-do which reduced both the frequency and the severity of the illness. Nevertheless mortality from tuberculosis undoubtedly declined in the middle and upper classes, as in the population as a whole, long before the introduction of effective treatment in 1947. It declined because the disease had become less prevalent in the community as a result of a general advance in nutrition. Thus well-to-do people benefited from a secondary effect of improved nutrition, for which they themselves offered little scope.

A second possibility is that there was some reduction of exposure to infection, particularly in early childhood. For the newborn the cleanliness of food is critical, and while the children of the aristocracy no doubt had sufficient food, the hygiene probably left a good deal to be desired. The transfer of the care of infants to

78

wet-nurses meant that their standards were often little better than those of the population at large. Although the condition of water supplies did not improve until the second half of the nineteenth century, and the cleanliness of food not until the beginning of the twentieth, it is possible that the standards of personal hygiene of well-to-do people improved from the late eighteenth century; certainly they had use of amenities such as water-closets long before they became available to the general public. But these suggestions are inevitably tentative, and it is questionable whether it will ever be possible to be confident about social class differences in health experience before they can be verified in national statistics.

B

HYGIENE

Second only to nutritional influences, in time and probably in importance, were the improvements in hygiene introduced progressively from the second half of the nineteenth century. They were the predominant reasons for the decline of water- and food-borne diseases, which were associated with about a fifth of the reduction of mortality from all causes between the mid nineteenth century and the present day (Table 3.2). The questions related to this influence which need a little further attention are its timing, its character, and its contribution.

For the period since cause of death was registered we are on fairly secure ground in dating the advance from the eighth decade (in England and Wales; it was somewhat later in most other countries). The decline of deaths from intestinal infections began at this time, and coincided with improvements in water supplies and sewage disposal initiated by sanitary reformers. There are no data which enable us to judge the trend of intestinal infections before registration of cause of death (1838); but with an expanding population, hygiene is unlikely to have advanced in the eighteenth century, and after the movement to towns, with uncontrolled living and working conditions, it must have deteriorated. Hence we can be fairly confident that reduction of exposure to infection, through better hygiene, was delayed until the 1870s, although there may well have been some improvement as a secondary consequence of the declining prevalence of disease at an earlier period.

There is also little doubt about the character of the hygienic measures. In the nineteenth century there were no substantial improvements in working and living conditions, and the main advances were in control of water and sewage. From about 1900 these measures were greatly extended by food hygiene, affecting most critically the quality of milk. Before that time it was not possible to protect milk from micro-organisms, and the rapid fall of deaths from gastro-enteritis which contributed substantially to the decline of infant mortality, was due largely to the introduction of sterilization, bottling, and safe transport of milk. These measures have of course been extended greatly in the present century, by improvements in working and living conditions, taking the latter to include advances (such as control of atmospheric pollution) in the community at large as well as in domestic circumstances.

The improvements in hygiene were the predominant reasons for the decline of water- and food-borne diseases. The rapid fall of deaths from intestinal infections owed little or nothing to immunization or therapy; and while it is never possible to say confidently that there has been no change in the relation between infective organisms and their hosts, it is most unlikely that the decline was influenced significantly by modification of the character of the diseases. Indeed if there has been a change, as noted above it is more probable that the populations in developed countries are now less resistant (in so far as resistance is determined by their genes) than in the past, since they are rarely exposed to organisms which cause intestinal infections.

IMMUNIZATION AND THERAPY

The conclusion that medical measures had little effect on the death-rate before 1935, and since then have been less important than other influences, merits further consideration in relation to two questions. First, what has been the impact of the notable advances in immunization and therapy in the twentieth century which are so highly valued? And second, is the contribution of medicine more impressive when account is taken of the effect on morbidity

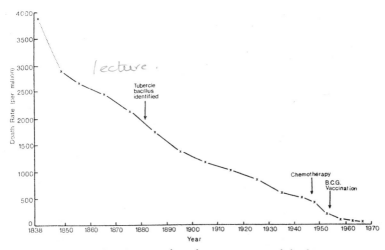

FIGURE 6.1. Respiratory tuberculosis: mean annual death-rates (standardized to 1901 population): England and Wales.

and disability as well as mortality? I shall consider briefly what are widely regarded as among the most remarkable advances: treatment of tuberculosis by streptomycin, and of pneumonia by sulphonamides and antibiotics; and immunization against tuberculosis, whooping cough, measles, and poliomyelitis.

Tuberculosis. A large part of the decline of the death-rate from tuberculosis in England and Wales occurred before the introduction of streptomycin in 1947 (Fig. 6.1). However, to assess its contribution we need to examine more closely the trend of mortality in the years immediately before and after it came into use. Since experience of the disease varies by age and sex, death-rates since 1921 are shown separately for males and females in three age-groups: under 15; 15–44; and 45 and over (Figs 6.2 and 6.3). Straight lines have been fitted to the rates for the years 1921 to 1946, and extrapolated to 1971, allowing for the slight increase between 1946 and 1947.

On the assumption that without streptomycin the decline of mortality would have continued at about the same rate as between 1921 and 1946, estimates have been made of the contribution of

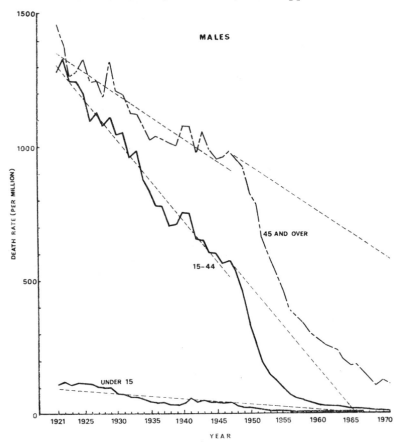

FIGURE 6.2. Respiratory tuberculosis: annual death-rates of males:
England and Wales.

treatment. The results are given in Table 6.1, for the sexes combined. Treatment by streptomycin reduced the number of deaths
in the period since it was introduced (1948–71) by 51 per cent; for
the total period since cause of death was first recorded (1848–71)
the reduction was 3·2 per cent.

Pneumonia. It would probably be agreed that the contribution of
sulphonamides and antibiotics can be examined most satisfactorily

82

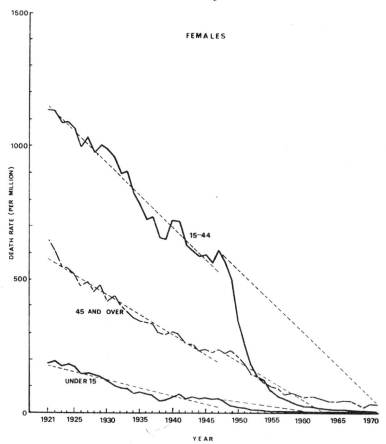

FIGURE 6.3. Respiratory tuberculosis: annual death-rates of females:
England and Wales.

TABLE 6.1. *Estimated number of deaths from respiratory tuberculosis
prevented by use of chemotherapy: England and Wales.*

	1948–1971	1848–1971
Estimated by extrapolation*	273,727	4,377,265
Actual	133,891	4,237,429
Deaths prevented	139,836	139,836
Proportion of deaths prevented	51%	3·2%

* Of 1921–46 rates.

83

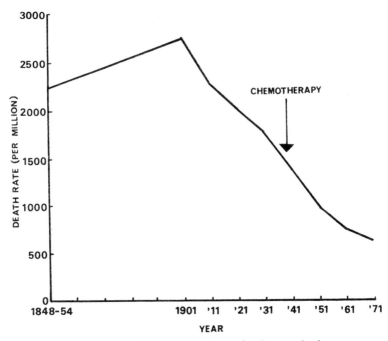

FIGURE 6.4. Bronchitis, pneumonia, and influenza: death-rates
(standardized to 1901 population): England and Wales.

in relation to mortality from certain respiratory infections, particularly pneumonia. Unfortunately pneumonia deaths cannot be
separated clearly from those due to bronchitis and influenza, at
least until quite recently. Mortality from the three diseases increased in the late nineteenth century, but declined from about
1900 (Fig. 6.4). Three-quarters of the subsequent reduction
occurred before the introduction of sulphapyridine (which was
effective against lobar pneumonia) and the figures provides no
convincing evidence that sulphanomides or antibiotics affected
the trend.

A more satisfactory approach is to consider the impact of
chemotherapy on the pneumonia death-rate, about which we can
be more confident in recent years. Figs 6.5 and 6.6. show the rates

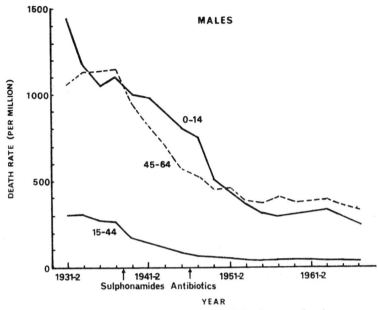

FIGURE 6.5. Pneumonia: mean annual death-rates of males:
England and Wales.

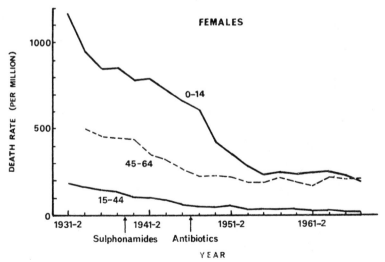

FIGURE 6.6. Pneumonia: mean annual death-rates of females:
England and Wales.

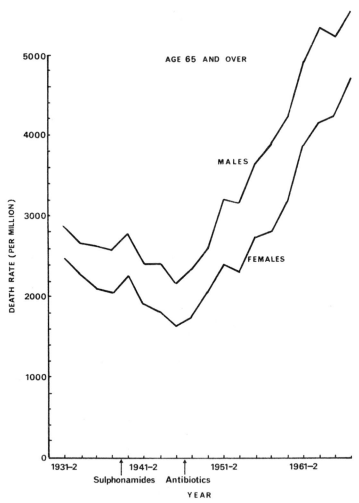

FIGURE 6.7. Pneumonia: mean annual death-rates: England and Wales.

for males and females respectively in three age-groups; there is evidence of a reduction of mortality at ages 0–14 and 45–64, but little or no effect at 15–44. However there has been a sharp increase in the death-rate for both sexes at ages 65 and over, from about the time when the antibiotics came into use (Fig. 6.7). The

86

rise was not due to an increase in numbers at the highest ages and seems much too great to be explained by transfer to pneumonia of deaths formerly attributed to other causes.

The increase in pneumonia deaths at late ages needs further investigation. But taken as a whole the evidence suggests that although chemotherapy had a moderate effect on mortality at ages 0–14 and 45–64, the effect on deaths at all ages was not large and was certainly not the main reason for the continued decline of the death-rate which was well established from the beginning of the century.

BCG vaccination. Since BCG has been used over much the same period as streptomycin in England and Wales, it is not possible to separate the effects of the two measures. Indeed in the examination of the trend of mortality from tuberculosis (above) it was assumed that the benefit was due wholly to streptomycin. That this assumption is not unreasonable is evident from the experience of the Netherlands, which has never had a national BCG vaccination programme but nevertheless had the lowest death-rates from respiratory tuberculosis for any European country in 1957–9 and 1967–9 (Fig. 6.8).

Immunization against whooping cough and measles. Since mortality from whooping cough and measles had fallen to a low level before immunization was used on a substantial scale in England and Wales, the effectiveness of the procedures must be judged in relation to morbidity, of which the best evidence is the frequency of notifications. Notification of the diseases began in 1940, but was very deficient for the first four years. The trend of notification rates since that time is shown for whooping cough and measles in Figs 6.9 and 6.10 respectively. Since the rate varies somewhat from year to year the figures are based on mean values for consecutive years.

The effect of immunization on whooping cough notifications is to some extent still in dispute. The rate has fallen almost continuously since 1950; but unfortunately, for the purposes of interpretation, immunization tends to be introduced gradually, and it is difficult to be certain when it was first used extensively. However

but ...

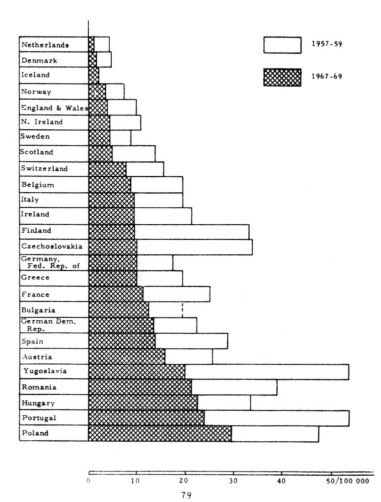

Deaths from Tuberculosis
(per 100,000)

| | 1957-59 |
| | 1967-69 |

Netherlands
Denmark
Iceland
Norway
England & Wales
N. Ireland
Sweden
Scotland
Switzerland
Belgium
Italy
Ireland
Finland
Czechoslovakia
Germany, Fed. Rep. of
Greece
France
Bulgaria
German Dem. Rep.
Spain
Austria
Yugoslavia
Romania
Hungary
Portugal
Poland

0   10   20   30   40   50/100 000

FIGURE 6.8. Tuberculosis: death-rates (per 100,000).

Sources: *World Health Statistics Report*, **23,** no. 8 (1970);
World Health Statistics Annual, **1** (1970).

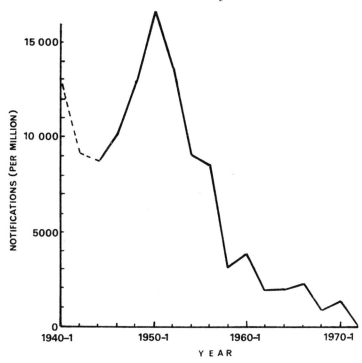

FIGURE 6.9. Whooping cough: mean annual notification rates
(per million persons under 15): England and Wales.

the references in the Annual Report of the Chief Medical Officer
suggest that the procedure was not in general use until at least a
few years after the onset of the decline of notifications.

The same appears to be true of measles. The notification rate
fell from 1950 to 1956, was more or less constant until about 1960,
and declined rapidly from that time. It was not until mid 1968
that vaccination was used on a national scale and less than a
quarter of all children had been immunized by the end of 1972.

Immunization against poliomyelitis. Any appraisal of medical
measures would be incomplete if it did not consider vaccination
against poliomyelitis, widely regarded as among the most impressive achievements of medical science. Since the number of

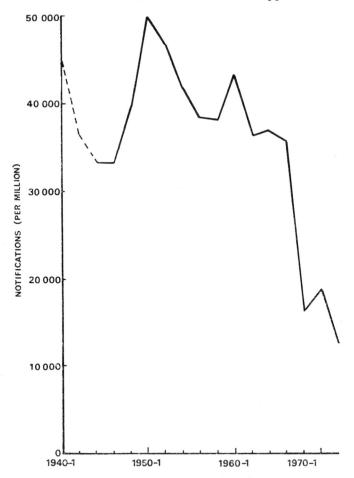

FIGURE 6.10. Measles: mean annual notification rates
(per million persons under 15): England and Wales.

deaths from the disease was very small, their reduction made little
contribution to the decline of the death-rate from all causes
(Chapter 3). However, the disabling effects of poliomyelitis are so
serious that the trend of notifications is much more important than
in most other infectious diseases.

90

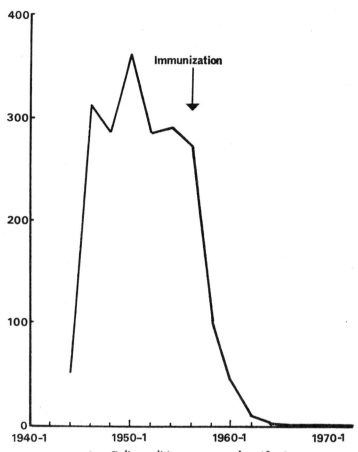

FIGURE 6.11. Poliomyelitis: mean annual notification rates
(per million persons under 15): England and Wales.

It is shown in Fig. 6.11. The rate fell sharply from 1956 to 1957,
and by 1964–5 there were few cases in England and Wales. For
this disease at least, national use of the vaccine was early enough
(1956) to make it reasonable to believe that immunization was
responsible for the reduction of notifications and prevention of
disabilities and deaths.

This appraisal of some of the most important medical advances leaves little doubt that their impact was much smaller than is generally supposed. The infections were declining long before effective measures were introduced, and since that time, with the notable exceptions of streptomycin and poliomyelitis vaccine, they have been less important than other influences. It is particularly significant that some procedures which were carefully assessed by randomized controlled trials (for example BCG vaccination) have not had the expected effects. The conclusion which seems inescapable is that the influences which determine man's experience of infectious disease (genetic, nutritional, environmental, and behavioural as well as medical) are complex, and we need to be very cautious when assuming that we understand the infections, or that we have in our hands the certain means of their control.

Finally I should consider briefly the possibility that the impact of medical measures has been much greater on morbidity than on mortality. Certainly it is true that we get little information from death certificates about the large number of diseases which cause sickness and disability but do not kill. Yet in spite of the deficiencies of evidence a few tentative conclusions can be drawn.

There have undoubtedly been considerable advances in the treatment of many uncomfortable and, sometimes, disabling conditions, such as hernias, piles, varicose veins, and arthritic hips. However, there is little evidence of substantial improvement in respect of many other non-lethal diseases such as mental subnormality, most psychiatric illnesses, and the common cold. It is also clear that there has been a large reduction of morbidity in association with the decline of deaths, for example from tuberculosis and other airborne infections. We are therefore unlikely to be seriously misled in using the trend of mortality as the main yardstick of the improvement in human health.

BEHAVIOUR

The other influence which contributed to the modern transformation of health was the change in reproductive behaviour which led to the decline of the birth-rate. The significance of this change

can hardly be exaggerated; without it the advances which followed the improvement in nutrition would in time, and on an evo-
lutionary scale very short time, have been eliminated. In England
and Wales, for example, if the birth-rate had continued at its
earlier level, the population today would be about 140 rather than
50 million. The effects on health and welfare can be imagined.
While, therefore, the initial progress was due to other influences,
the change in reproductive practices which restricted numbers was
the essential complement without which the advance would soon
have been reversed.

But the restraint on reproduction also had a direct effect on
mortality. If infanticide had the significance which has been
suggested, the virtual elimination of this important cause of death
in advanced countries was due mainly to avoidance of unwanted
pregnancies. Indeed as noted previously, it is quite possible that
this behavioural change made the largest contribution to the
decline of non-infective causes of death.

It would be unwise to attempt to express numerically the contribution which the different influences have made to the decline of
mortality. There are too many unknowns. We do not know the
causes of death in the eighteenth and early nineteenth centuries, so
conclusions for that time are in the nature of informed guesses. In
the post-registration period the Registrar-General's classification
includes some ill-defined and heterogeneous categories (such as
'prematurity, immaturity, other diseases of infancy' and 'old age')
whose composition is far from clear. And it is not possible to
estimate with any precision the contribution which therapeutic
and other advances have made to the decline of the multiple non-
infective causes of death which together were associated with
about a quarter of the reduction of mortality in this century.

With due regard for these and other grounds for reservation.
I believe it is possible to draw a few general conclusions concerning
the main influences.

1. Improvement in nutrition was the earliest, and, over the whole
period since about 1700, the most important influence.

2. Hygienic measures were responsible for at least a fifth of the reduction of the death-rate between the mid nineteenth century and today. This is the proportion of the decline which was associated with water- and food-borne diseases.

3. With the exception of vaccination against smallpox, whose contribution was small, the influence of immunization and therapy on the death-rate was delayed until the twentieth century, and had little effect on national mortality trends before the introduction of sulphonamides in 1935. Since that time it has not been the only, or probably the most important influence.

4. The change in reproductive practice which led to the decline of the birth-rate was also very significant, since it ensured that the improvement in health brought about by other means was not reversed by rising numbers.

If we group together the advances in nutrition and hygiene as environmental measures, the influences responsible for the decline of mortality and associated improvement in health were environmental, behavioural, and therapeutic. They became effective from the eighteenth, nineteenth, and twentieth centuries respectively and their order in time was also that of their effectiveness.

INFLUENCES ON HEALTH TODAY

The appraisal of influences on health in the past suggests that we owe the improvement, not to what happens when we are ill, but to the fact that we do not so often become ill; and we remain well, not because of specific measures such as vaccination and immunization, but because we enjoy a higher standard of nutrition and live in a healthier environment. In at least one important respect, reproduction, we also behave more responsibly.

However it by no means follows that these influences have the same relative importance today as in the past. In technologically advanced countries the decline of the infections has been followed by a vast change in the character of health problems; and even in developing countries it is possible that the influences have been modified by advances in medical science and in science and technology in general. It will therefore be desirable to examine briefly the nature of the residual health problems which have become predominant as the infections have declined. They are broadly in four classes.

RESIDUAL HEALTH PROBLEMS

Congenital. Congenital diseases and disabilities are those present at birth, although some, such as malformations of the heart, may not be recognized until later. They comprise two of the four classes identified in Chapter 2 (p. 27): a small number due to disorders of single genes or chromosomes; and a much larger number which are multifactorial, and presumably arise from hazards associated with implantation and early embryonic development. As would be expected, these conditions have been relatively unresponsive to the improvements which have been so successful after birth, and there has been no significant reduction in the incidence of major handicaps such as mental defect and congenital malformations. Most deaths in childhood are now associated with conditions which have been present from birth.

Within that part of the future which it is realistic to discuss here, there is little prospect of reducing substantially the incidence of congenital diseases and disabilities, by modification of genes, by identification of parents whose offspring are likely to be affected, or by removal of the intra-uterine hazards which appear to be responsible for most congenital abnormalities. The serious ones are also unlikely to be corrected by treatment. The most promising approach is recognition of the conditions during pregnancy and their elimination by abortion. There is considerable scope for improvement of obstetric care before and during delivery, but this is mainly to protect the mother and normal infant rather than to correct the disability of the abnormal one.

This short appraisal suggests that the measures likely to be effective with congenital diseases and disabilities are quite different from those that have been successful in post-natal life. They depend largely on direct intervention. This is not to say that adequate food and a safe environment are no longer important. But where they can be taken for granted, as they largely can in favoured sections of the populations of technologically advanced countries, the solution of the congenital problems which remain will probably depend mainly on a physico-chemical approach.

(2) *Geriatric.* The diseases of late life are in two of the four classes listed in Chapter 2 (p. 27). Both are multifactorial but one (associated with the wearing-out of organs at the end of life) appears to be determined at fertilization, whereas the other is not. The former cannot be expected to respond to environmental modifications; the latter, in principle, might do so.

These conclusions are consistent with the trends of the past century or more, when the volume of medical problems associated with ageing has increased enormously. There are three reasons: the increase in the number of old people, due to the reduction of mortality in early life and the decline of the birth-rate; the intractability of disorders of late life which are determined at fertilization; and an increase in the frequency of certain diseases (chronic bronchitis, coronary artery disease, and some cancers) due to unfavourable environmental influences, mainly of a behavioural kind.

There is clearly considerable scope for prevention of diseases of the last type, and for correction or relief of some other disabilities by medical treatment. However, the increase in expectation of life that can be expected is not large, and the aged who survive as a result of treatment (for example of cancer or heart disease) are not usually restored to full health. Hence a large and probably increasing proportion of medical work for the elderly consists of prolonged care of patients who are physically or mentally disabled.

(3) *Psychiatric.* More tentatively, it is suggested that many psychiatric conditions, at least in early and middle life, are probably in the fourth class referred to on p. 27; that is to say, they are not determined irreversibly at fertilization, and arise from influences which are mainly post-natal. The common forms have not responded to the measures which have been successful in reducing mortality. The virtual disappearance of tertiary syphilis, once a frequent cause of admission to psychiatric hospitals, is the best-documented exception, and while the evidence is less complete, it is probable that illnesses associated with toxic and nutritional hazards have also declined. But with such exceptions, the common forms of neurotic, psychotic, and psychosomatic conditions appear to be as prevalent as formerly.

Opinion is so widely divided about the nature of mental illness that it is unrealistic to expect agreement about the measures on which control will depend. The gap is immeasurable between the psycho-analysts and those who believe it is practicable to seek a physical or chemical solution to major psychiatric problems. However I believe it is agreed that the volume and types of mental (including psychosomatic) illness may differ considerably in different populations and in the same population at different times. Remarkable examples are the variation in incidence of peptic ulcer in countries of western Europe, and the change in the male/female ratio of deaths due to perforation from peptic ulcer in New York City during this century (from 1 to 1 to about 20 to 1). There are also some striking differences in hospital admission rates of schizophrenics, for example between native-born and 'new' Australians (those who have emigrated from Europe).

This is slender evidence on which to base a general conclusion concerning methods needed in mental illness. But past experience at least indicates that not much can be expected from 'more of the same', from better nutrition and removal of physical hazards. The variation in experience of different societies suggests that social institutions and behaviour contribute largely to the occurrence of psychological illness, and if so it is to their modification that we must look for prevention and control.

(4) *Other diseases which are potentially preventable.* Finally, there are many non-psychiatric conditions which arise in early and middle life. They are almost all in the fourth class (p. 27), polygenic and attributable to post-natal influences. They include, of course, the infections, whose decline as a result of nutritional and hygienic improvements provides striking evidence of their environmental origins. But most other diseases and disabilities (for example, diabetes, accidents, peptic ulcer, rheumatoid arthritis, and many cancers) are probably of the same type, and differ from the infections only in the greater difficulty in recognizing the hazards and bringing them under control. A very large part of medical (and dental) work today, including some of the most successful, is concerned with conditions such as accidents, diabetes, and dental caries which are essentially preventable.

97

RESIDUAL INFLUENCES ON HEALTH

The review of past improvements in health suggested that the main influences, in order of time and importance, were environmental (nutrition and hygiene), behavioural (control of reproduction), and medical (immunization and therapy). To what extent has this order been affected by the modification of health problems?

The main change is that in developed countries behavioural influences are now relatively more important than environmental ones. The reasons are fairly clear. Today, as in the past, the scope for improvement is greatest in respect of diseases which are not determined irreversibly at fertilization, and whose appearance is due to post-natal influences. The diseases which declined in the past were the infections, on which the significant influences were nutritional and hygienic. They could therefore be controlled by external measures which were made effective by public action. But the diseases which are conspicuous after the decline of the infections are determined largely by human behaviour and could be controlled only by its modification.

Behavioural influences. If limitation of numbers is no longer so critical in developed countries, internationally it remains an important, perhaps the most important, requirement for improvement in health. However, the conclusion that behaviour is now predominant rests also on the significance of another class of influences: personal behaviour in relation to smoking, exercise, diet, etc.

There is little doubt about the reasons why these features of behaviour have become so important; smoking, sedentary living, and consumption of excess food or of refined foods, are all profound departures from the conditions under which man evolved. Moreover the changes are very recent: refined foods became widely available in the early nineteenth century; sedentary living dates from the introduction of the motor-car; and smoking on a significant scale has occurred only in the last few decades. In time, no doubt, man could adapt by natural selection to these as to other changes during his evolution; but adaptation cannot take

TABLE 6.2. *Increase in expectation of life of males in the period 1838–54 to 1970.**

Age	Non-smokers	Smokers of 25+ CPD
0	31·9	26·0
25	13·2	7·0
35	10·3	4·1
45	7·4	2·1
55	4·6	0·6
65	2·3	0·3

*Based on mortality experience of (a) British doctors, smokers and non-smokers and (b) estimates of life expectation of males in England and Wales in 1838–54 and 1970.

place quickly and will not occur at all without extensive early mortality among the susceptible.

Although the relative importance of behaviour and other influences cannot be estimated accurately, it is possible to assess the ill-effects of one major feature, namely smoking. Table 6.2 shows, for smokers (25 cigarettes daily and over) and non-smokers of various ages, the increase in expectation of life which occurred between 1838–54 and 1970. From age 25 the increase for smokers was about half or less than half of the increase for non-smokers. This result can be interpreted to mean that in the past century the improvement in expectation of life of mature males *from all causes* has been reduced by at least half by smoking alone. The fact that so large a reduction has been associated with a single practice indicates that in technologically advanced countries behavioural influences are now more important than all others.

Environmental influences. Throughout the world deficient food remains a serious problem and even in the wealthiest countries there are sections of the population which are inadequately, to be distinguished from unwisely, fed. Because the deficiency is determined mainly by economic conditions rather than by the individual's personal choice, it is classified here as an environmental rather than a behavioural influence.

The second class of environmental problems comprises the hazards in the physical environment. A distinction must of course be made between developing countries, where control has only recently begun, and developed countries where a great deal has been achieved during the past century. Even so, many well recognized risks associated with atmosphere, housing, traffic, insect vectors, and working conditions are far from being eliminated, while others inherent in contemporary life have not been fully assessed or even, in some cases, recognized.

Immunization and therapy. An attempt will be made in Chapter 9 to consider more carefully the potential contribution of medical measures. Here it need only be noted that in the foreseeable future they cannot be expected to make so large a contribution to prevention of sickness and premature death as the other main influences.

In the light of these conclusions the requirements for health can be stated simply. Those fortunate enough to be born free of significan congenital disease or disability will remain well if three basic needs are met: they must be adequately fed; they must be protected from a wide range of hazards in the environment; and they must not depart radically from the pattern of personal behaviour under which man evolved, for example by smoking, overeating, or sedentary living.

This interpretation suggests that what is true for other living things is true also for man, namely that health depends primarily on control of environmental influences, including those which the individual makes for himself by his behaviour. It is not difficult to see why this should be so. The only diseases and disabilities that are inevitable are those determined irreversibly at fertilization. So defined they comprise conditions due to single genes or chromosomal aberrations, and some associated with ageing and death. The large majority of live births have not been programmed genetically in such a way that disease is inevitable, at least until they reach late life, and sickness and premature death are determined essentially by environmental influences. Of course prenatal hazards are relatively inaccessible, and the response to the environment depends on genetic constitution. Nevertheless an individual. however prone, will not acquire tuberculosis unless he encounters the tubercle bacillus, just as, however gifted, he will never become a concert pianist unless at an early age he has access to a piano.

Part Two

The role of medicine

7

Health services

In Part One the determinants of man's health were assessed in two ways: first, by examining conceptually the role of heredity and environment in the aetiology of disease (Chapter 2); and second, by appraisal of influences on health which have operated in the past and, having regard to the change in disease problems, can be expected to operate in future (Chapters 3–6). The conclusions derived from these different approaches are broadly consistent.

1. Most diseases, and particularly the common ones, are not inevitable. They result from environmental influences on genetic material which is varied, complex, and, at present, little understood. In relation to the feasibility of preventing common diseases, the important issue is neither the understanding of genetic mechanisms nor the balance sheet of nature and nurture, which in any case cannot be quantified accurately; it is the practicability of controlling the environmental component. The most significant distinction is between prenatal influences which are relatively intractable and post-natal influences many of which can be modified or removed.

2. This theoretical interpretation is in accord with past experience. The improvement in health since the eighteenth century was in respect of post-natal rather than prenatal conditions, and was associated predominantly with the infections, the diseases most susceptible to control. The influences which led to their predominance from the time of the first Agricultural Revolution 10,000 years ago were insufficient food, environmental hazards, and excessive numbers, and the measures which led to their decline from the time of the modern Agricultural and Industrial Revolutions were predictably improved nutrition, better hygiene, and contraception. These advances preceded effective medical intervention in the form of immunization and therapy which has made only a small contribution to the reduction of mortality and morbidity associated with infectious diseases.

3. The change in the character of health problems which followed the decline of the infections in developed countries has not invalidated the conclusion that most diseases, both physical and mental, are associated with influences which in principle might be controlled. But relatively more of these influences are now prenatal, and among post-natal influences those which the individual determines by his own behaviour (smoking, eating, exercise, and the like) are more important than those which depend mainly on action by society: provision of essential food and protection from hazards. The contribution to be expected from personal medical measures to the prevention of sickness and premature death remains tertiary, in relation to the predominant behavioural and environmental influences.

The disposal of society's investment in health is based on quite different premises. It is assumed that we are ill and are made well, whereas it is nearer the truth to say that we are well and are made ill. Few people think of themselves as having the major responsibility for their own health, and the enormous resources which technologically advanced countries assign to the health field are used mainly to treat disease or, to a lesser extent, to prevent it by personal measures such as immunization.

The conclusion that the predominant influences are quite different from those that have hitherto been assumed clearly has implications for health-related services. However before examining them I should comment on the time likely to be required to bring about adjustments. In consideration of health services there is a tendency to think on too small a time-scale, and this is particularly evident in the United States where it often seems difficult to interest planners in any proposal unlikely to appeal to Congress within the next eighteen months (less if the Administration is about to change). It should be remembered that in most advanced countries the contemporary pattern of health services had its origins in the hospitals built in the eighteenth century, and is based on concepts established much earlier. We can hardly be surprised if some decades are required to modify an approach which has developed over hundreds of years.

Furthermore, a different concept of the basis of human health should not be thought of as a recipe for action whose validity is to be judged by whether it provides an immediate solution to some of the most complex problems facing society: for example, in developing countries limitation of numbers and provision of food, and in developed countries modification of behaviour and a fresh approach to personal health services based on recognition of the limited scope for therapeutic intervention and the predominance of the need for care. The enlarged understanding of health and disease should rather be regarded as a conceptual base, whose implications for services, education, and research will need to be developed progressively over a considerable period. It is therefore only a very preliminary examination of these matters which can be attempted in this chapter and the two that follow.

NUTRITION

In considering health-related services I shall begin with nutrition, which internationally is probably still the most important determinant of health. The grounds on which lack of food is regarded as the main influence in developing countries today and in all countries in the recent past were summarized in Chapter 6. The evidence is essentially circumstantial, but in this it resembles the evidence for the operation of natural selection and is not on that account necessarily less convincing.

For developing countries of Asia, Africa, and Latin America, the conclusion concerning nutrition is in accord with so much recent experience that it is unnecessary to dwell on its implications at length. It is well recognized that it is essential to increase food supplies, and since they cannot be expanded very rapidly or indefinitely it is also necessary to restrict numbers. This of course was Malthus's central idea, or, perhaps more accurately, the deduction which follows from it, outlined in the opening chapter of his *Essay on Population* and stated succinctly on its first page: 'The tendency of all animated life is to increase beyond the nourishment provided for it.' The reception of this idea was coloured by reaction to the religious, social, and political opinions with which he associated it, and by well-founded doubts about the validity of his conclusion that food supplies increase arithmetically whereas populations tend to increase geometrically. The fact remains that Malthus associated the two basic notions of food deficiency and excessive numbers, and it is most unfortunate that subsequently they became dissociated in concept and practice, largely because of religious taboos on contraception. Happily the religious objections are being gradually withdrawn, and international organizations are at last permitted to include family planning among their objectives. It should be linked so far as possible to food policies, and the related issues of improved nutrition and limitation of population growth should be given the priority they merit on the grounds that they are not only of general importance to man's welfare, but are also the major determinants of health.

The significance of food in developed countries is of course somewhat different. There it can be assumed that most people have enough to eat, and the more usual problem is consumption of excessive or ill-balanced diets. Since this is determined by personal choice as well as by custom and public policy, it should be regarded as a behavioural influence on health. However, even in the wealthiest countries there are sections of the population which are still inadequately, as distinct from unwisely fed. In proportion and composition they probably vary from one country to another, but in Britain today they are mainly in two classes, the late children of large families and elderly people, particularly those who are living alone.

There is of course general concern about the welfare of such groups, and in Britain efforts are made to assist them, for example by family allowances, Home Helps, and Meals-on-Wheels. Nevertheless they do not have the attention they would be given if it were recognized that food is critical to their health. Nor do they receive the kind of assistance that would be most useful, for example food supplements and subsidies such as were provided during the Second World War, and whose effectiveness was reflected in health indices in spite of deterioration in some other features of working and living conditions. If a choice must be made, free school meals are more important for the health of poor children than immunization programmes, and both are more effective than hospital beds.

The potential significance of food subsidies to health is still unrecognized. They were introduced under the exigencies of the war period as a device for restricting the cost of living, and it is hardly noticed that society has stumbled on to an efficient instrument for the promotion of health. Indeed it is often assumed that in an affluent society cheap food may be positively harmful ('Beyond a certain point more and better food appears to mean increased need for medical services'[1]) and there are some grounds for this conclusion under present economic policies which take little or no account of their impact on health. We subsidize sugar which is harmful, and make butter which contains saturated fats competitive in price with the more innocuous margarine. The cost of refined flour, remarkably, is as low or lower than that of whole meal, and the health conscious individual who seeks to restore the fibre to his diet by the addition of bran will find that this simple commodity, which was cheap so long as it was fed only to pets and livestock, has become expensive since it was shown to be of value to man.

Having regard for the importance of food to health, the aim of public policy should be to use supplements and subsidies discriminately to put essential constituents within the reach of everyone, and to provide inducements for people to prefer foods that are beneficial to those that are harmful. Of course these aims cannot be expected to exclude all other considerations, such as international agreements and the solvency of farmers who have been encouraged to produce livestock and dairy products rather than grains. Nevertheless in all future evaluations of agricultural and related economic policies, the health implications should be given a primary place.

BEHAVIOUR

The behavoural change most significant for health in the past was the limitation of family size which led to restriction of numbers. This influence is critical in developing countries today, and is still important in many developed countries whose populations have not yet achieved a rate of growth consistent with the needs of health and welfare. Nevertheless in the advanced countries it is on modification of personal habits such as smoking and sedentary living that health primarily depends.

1. Galbraith, J. K., *The Affluent Society* (Penguin Books, 1969), p. 209.

This bring us to one of the most sensitive areas of discussion related to the health field. Many people who can accept the need for public intervention in food policies, control of environment, and provision of medical care are deeply suspicious of attempts to modify personal behaviour. Our habits commonly begin as pleasures of which we have no need and end as necessities in which we have no pleasure. Nevertheless we tend to resent the suggestion that anyone should try to change them, even on the disarming grounds that they do so for our own good.

Two objections are often raised to the suggestion that behaviour should be modified by public action: that this would be an unreasonable intrusion on the rights of the individual; and that any such attempt would be certain to fail. These objections will be examined more closely, with special reference to smoking which epitomizes the problem and the difficulties.

On the first point, it is said that the individual must be free to choose whether he wishes to smoke. But he is not free; with a drug of addiction the option is open only at the beginning, so that the critical decision to smoke is taken, not by consenting adults but by children below the age of consent. The question confronting society is not therefore whether smoking by addicts should be prohibited; it is whether it is acceptable to induce children to become addicts at an age when they neither know nor much care about the associated risks.

The same logic should be applied to other aspects of personal behaviour which are known to be important to health. It is not suggested that we should be required to exercise, to limit consumption of alcohol, sugar, and dairy products, and to avoid self-prescribed drugs and some of the physician-prescribed variety, beneficial as all these measures would undoubtedly be for our health. But it is not inconsistent with respect for personal freedom to attempt to create an environment which encourages people to do what is good for them and to avoid what is bad. It seems particularly reprehensible to do the reverse, to seek ways to induce children to damage their health by smoking for no other purpose than to sustain profits.

The conclusion that personal habits cannot be modified by acceptable public action is I think mistaken, and arises largely from the application of too short a time-scale. The physician says, 'I have not so far succeeded in persuading many, perhaps any, of my patients to give up tobacco', and he concludes that smoking habits are unchanged. Nevertheless they are visibly changing. As a lifelong non-smoker, or almost, having given up at the age of 6, for most of my life I have been a member of a depressed class. Not to smoke was often regarded as antisocial, and refusal of a cigarette at an awkward first meeting was considered equivalent to an unwillingness to shake hands. I now find myself frequently in situations where it would be as difficult to smoke as it was formerly not to, and where most of those present would be about as reluctant to light up in public as they would be to spit. It is not a valid objection that a change in smoking habits has so far been observed mainly in doctors, for refinements of behaviour usually begin with a sensitive or well-informed minority and spread gradually to others, an observation made by Frazer in the opening pages of *The Golden Bough*.

Moreover there is evidence that the general population is also affected. Not so long ago it was difficult to find a non-smoking compartment in a train and it was thought unreasonable to object to smoking in one. (How often one heard: 'You don't mind, do you dear?') Today half the accommodation of main-line trains in Britain is reserved for non-smokers and I have the impression that they are the most crowded compartments. Not half the adult population are non-smokers, but more than half are already aware that it is unpleasant to sit in the presence of smokers.

The conclusion that behaviour changes, albeit over a longer time-scale than we might like, is well illustrated by experience of contraception. Before 1800 there was no convincing evidence that human beings would ever restrict their reproduction on a significant scale, yet by the end of the century birth-rates were falling throughout the western world. That change also began among well-informed people, but extended gradually to all sections of the population. With this evidence of modification of one of the most intimate features of behaviour there is no reason to doubt that in time other practices which are critical to health will also change.

However much thought needs to be given to the means by which such changes can be brought about. The usual approach through advertisements, posters, and public exhortations seems much too superficial, and takes little account of the profound influences which are shaping behaviour. It is questionable whether advertisements ever led anyone to become a smoker or an alcoholic, their main influence being on the amount smoked or on the selection of a particular fag or tipple. Indeed the effect of professional advertising is probably trivial in relation to that of the variety provided gratuitously by press and television. Even the most responsible newspapers have no hesitation in exhibiting some of the most admired figures of our time with cigarettes in their hands or mouths. On 11 April 1976, the *Sunday Times* devoted nearly half a page to a photograph of Glenda Jackson as 'The Abbess', which seemed to symbolize divine as well as social sanction for the lighted cigarette suspended limply from the corner of her mouth. With unsolicited support of this kind it would not be surprising if the tobacco companies regarded their vigorous defence of paid advertising as no more than a minor skirmish designed to divert attention from the significance of the main event.

Yet if a distinguished actress cannot be persuaded to give up smoking for her own good, she might accept that she should not prejudice the health of her admirers, who include young children, by displaying her addiction in public. The same appeal might be addressed to doctors on behalf of their patients and to parents on behalf of their children. Clearly there is no general answer to the diverse problems associated with modification of behaviour except perhaps that they should be considered individually and with imagination as well as tact. Broadly what is needed is a change in way of life rather than a commentary on it, which is all that is achieved by some of the traditional methods of health education.

ENVIRONMENT

In their contribution to health in the past, the hygienic measures introduced progressively from the second half of the nineteenth century were second only to nutrition. Their importance is well recognized, and the question is now whether there are additional steps that need to be taken in the light of conclusions concerning the determinants of health in the present day.

Public responsibility for health services was introduced in the mid nineteenth century primarily for the purpose of dealing with infectious diseases, and the measures initially taken were control of the physical environment and provision of services, including hospitals, for infectious patients. The new service, based on local authorities was preventive in outlook and emphasized improvements in the environment as a means of promoting health. This viewpoint was reflected in the concept of the role of the medical officer of health who was conceived by Chadwick as 'a district medical officer independent of private practice and with the securities of special qualifications and responsibilities to initiate sanitary measures'. Duncan, the first medical officer of health (in Liverpool) was 'most intimately acquainted with the sanitary conditions of which he spoke and had long given intelligent and humane consideration to means of improving them'.[1]

In the present century the health work of local authorities was greatly extended, by development of personal health services (from 1906), by responsibility for public hospitals (from 1929 to 1948) and by duties related to the care and after care of the sick imposed by the National Health Service in 1948. But this extension did not remove their responsibility for environmental medicine; nor did it diminish their interest in the prevention of disease and promotion of health. The conspicuous disadvantage of traditional public health was its isolation from therapeutic services, provided since 1948 almost exclusively by other public authorities.

The 1974 reorganization eliminated this anomaly, but in unifying administration of personal medical services under the new regional and area authorities it separated them from environmental services which remain under local government. The medical specialist in environmental medicine now has a consultative rather than an executive role, and the specialist in community medicine, the heir to the public health tradition, is concerned largely with personal medical care. In such circumstances it seems important to ask whether environmental measures will receive

1. Simon, John, *English Sanitary Institutions* (London: Smith Elder and Co., 1897), p. 247.

the attention they deserve, and, more broadly, whether the new service will give due emphasis to the prevention of disease and promotion of health. Will the specialist in community medicine bring to the new administration the goals and outlook which characterized public health from its introduction in the nineteenth century? Or will the pressures of therapeutic services obscure these aims, until with a new generation of doctors who have never worked in public health they are finally forgotten?

The attitude of medicine to the environment has always been somewhat equivocal, and the Chief Scientist probably expressed the view of most educators when he wrote: 'the most characteristic function of a doctor lies in the diagnosis and treatment of disease in the individual patient' and 'the great majority of doctors will remain concerned with disease and not with "positive health" or "community medicine" or "social medicine" '.[1] This viewpoint is reflected in medical education, which gives little attention to environmental influences and measures needed for their control.

This approach might have been accepted, with reservations, when a special class of doctors was responsible for the prevention of disease and the promotion of health. But the specialist in community medicine is now concerned largely with personal health services, and it cannot be taken for granted that he will have the same influence on environmental medicine as his predecessor in public health. However it might be argued that such a change would not be serious, since the measures needed to improve the environment are already largely in the hands of non-medical people.

It is not easy for doctors to accept that medicine is not vitally concerned with the major determinants of health. However this reaction might be dismissed as professional chauvinism if there were no more tangible grounds for thinking that it is important to retain, and indeed to extend medical interest in investigation and control of hazards. These grounds are as follows.

In spite of improvements the environment still presents many and varied threats to health. They are more complex than in the

1. Black, D. A. K., *The Logic of Medicine* (Edinburgh and London: Oliver and Boyd, 1968).

past; for example, it was easier to recognize, measure, and control the risks of infected water and polluted air than those associated with drug therapy and radiological examination of the breast. Moreover, in a highly industrialized society, the risks are constantly changing.

Responsibility is already very fragmented, different administrations being concerned with measures related to: (*a*) occupation; (*b*) local issues such as housing, water supplies, and atmospheric pollution; (*c*) national issues such as air, rail, and road travel and pollution of sea and rivers; and (*d*) risks arising from medical investigation and treatment. The work associated with such large and complex problems must of course involve many administrations and professions, but it seems inevitable that there will be serious omissions so long as there is no organization, local as well as central, with a more comprehensive responsibility for surveillance.

It also seems essential to have a medical contribution. The scope of inquiry is greatly enlarged when it starts from an interest in disease problems as well as in environmental planning. Many examples could be cited to support the conclusion that medical interest is essential in identification and investigation of environmental influences on health, if not always in the measures needed to achieve control. It was a doctor's experience of cholera that led to investigation of the Broad Street pump; observations on the malformed resulted in recognition of the teratogenic effects of rubella and thalidomide; and a surgeon's awareness of the different disease patterns in Africans and Europeans drew attention to the significance of refinement of food to intestinal disease.

Under the reorganized National Health Service the medical role in environmental medicine is at least in danger of being weakened. Some of those working in this field will be only too pleased to be free of the medical yoke, and with medical responsibility focused more exclusively on services provided under the NHS, educators are quite likely to respond by concluding that the environment has no place in medical education. Even if environmental problems are assigned to a special class of doctors, it will be difficult for such a class to emerge if the subject finds no place in undergraduate training.

I suggest that at least three steps are necessary: strengthening of the medical role in environmental medicine, with appropriate developments in training; a more co-ordinated approach to the different hazards of the environment (occupational, domestic, iatrogenic, etc.) both centrally and locally; and a considered attack on the risks associated with medical investigation and treatment.

PERSONAL HEALTH SERVICES

The conclusion that medical intervention has made, and can be expected to make a relatively small contribution to prevention of sickness and death could not fail to have large implications for personal health services. They have evolved on quite different assumptions; treatment by surgery and drugs is widely regarded as the basis of health and the essence of medical care, and nearly half of the total expenditure in Britain (46·0 per cent in 1970/1) is on acute hospitals. These hospitals do not care for most sick people, of whom the large majority are in their own homes under general practitioners or in psychiatric, geriatric, or other institutions; if they are not having a substantial influence on health it is clearly desirable to reconsider their role.

There are many issues which arise from reappraisal of the determinants of health but I shall limit my comment to three which are particularly important: the relation between technology and care; the problem of ensuring the quality of care; and the relation between medically qualified and other health workers.

(1) TECHNOLOGY AND CARE

Since the eighteenth century medical activities have been divided broadly into favoured and depressed areas corresponding respectively to patients for whom it was thought something could be done and others, the large majority, for whom little could be done. This distinction had its origin in the admission policies of voluntary hospitals. Although their work was not originally restricted, from the eighteenth century it became increasingly concerned with short-term care. This made it necessary for public authorities to accept responsibility for other classes of patients.

In Britain the decision to make admission to an institution a condition of public assistance (in 1834) brought the large number of destitute sick under the Poor Law. They were accommodated in workhouses, supplemented later by infirmaries built as hospitals. But the infirmaries, following the example of the voluntary hospitals, restricted their admissions, and the medical care of the indigent was left to the mixed workhouse, the only institution unable to reject it. This grouping of a large heterogeneous class of patients who had in common only their destitution was the origin of the chronic hospital.

From the nineteenth century the mentally ill, also excluded from the voluntary hospitals, were admitted to county asylums. This separated them from the Poor Law, and led to a division of responsibility between asylum and workhouse which was the origin of the anomalous relationship between mental and chronic hospitals. Finally the establishment of acute psychiatric units in general hospitals further exaggerated the isolation of the mental hospital. The history of institutions for the mentally subnormal is in some respects parallel. This is the background of the most significant feature of hospitals, the separation of mental, chronic (now geriatric), and mental subnormality hospitals from general hospitals.

The distinction between hospitals had its parallel in a division of medical practice. The founding of voluntary hospitals from the eighteenth century, and of public hospitals from the nineteenth had two very significant effects: it changed what had been wholly a domiciliary service into one in which hospital work became increasingly important; and it replaced the long-standing divisions between physician, surgeon, and apothecary by another between general practitioner and consultant. Originally this distinction had little justification in their training and competence, and was determined mainly by their relationship to the hospital. In the words of the *British Medical Journal*, a consultant was 'a practitioner among the sick who could charge higher fees because he had a hospital appointment'. Even today, the consultant is distinguished from the general practitioner less by the subtlety of his treatment than by the strength of conviction with which he executes it.

The division of medical work into favoured and depressed areas which has existed since the eighteenth century is in danger of being extended by the growth of technology. Professional interest is increasingly absorbed by methods of investigation and treatment whose complexities seem to challenge the attention of the best minds and whose rewards are assumed to justify it. The acute hospital is likely to become still more selective in its admission policies, and the teaching centre with its concentration of resources and abilities, will be the most exclusive of all. Doctors, nurses, and other health workers would then be trained in an environment which reveals a very limited part of the health task, an environment where prestige, rewards, and professional interest all seem to point in the same direction. After qualification, understandably, they will seek to continue in the activities which were the focus of their training, and only with the greatest reluctance will they consent to enter the massive neglected areas of health care. The large numbers of patients, particularly among the congenitally handicapped, the mentally ill and the aged sick, whose disabilities are not thought to provide scope for technology, will be pushed further into the background, and the division of health services into two worlds will be even sharper than it is today.

Many people who regret this trend, and particularly the low standards of care for the majority of patients to which it leads, nevertheless think it is justified by the achievements of acute hospitals. They suggest that if a choice must be made it is better to treat appendicitis in a young adult before incontinence in an elderly person. However, such examples are entirely misleading. In the first place, mean age of admissions has risen in the past thirty years, and a comparison between patients in acute and other hospitals is now between the old and the old, rather than between the young and the old. Secondly, a successful operation which restores the patient to health is not typical of the work of acute hospitals, much of which is palliative or unproved. Thirdly, in what is unsatisfactorily referred to as the chronic sector there is scope for services which are as critical to health as any on the acute side. Consider, for example, the need to admit to an institution a hyperactive mentally retarded child who is destroying the health as well as the happiness of his family. Such children are to be found in every large town; yet their care is not regarded as urgent and is rarely given the priority it merits on health grounds.

Another and common reaction to the disparity in standards is the suggestion that it should be adjusted by a simple transfer of resources from acute to chronic care. But these terms are misleading, for patients do not fall sharply into two classes according to their need for technology or care; those in general hospitals need personal care, and many in mental, geriatic, and sub-normality hospitals would benefit from investigation and active treatment. Furthermore it should be remembered that with a population of hospital patients composed mainly of the elderly, as is the case today, the different phases of care (acute, rehabilitative, and prolonged) are required by the same people at different stages of their lives and sometimes at different stages of the same illness.

What is needed is not merely a transfer of resources between existing services, but a reappraisal of services (hospitals, medical practice, and community health and social services) in the light of the conclusion that the scope for effective therapeutic intervention is limited, and that the largest task confronting the personal health services is the care of patients, using that term in the widest sense to include (for example) active rehabilitation and terminal care as well as nursing and other services for patients with residual disabilities. In broad terms what is required is a framework which meets, and where necessary reconciles, the diverse need of technology and care. This aim is unlikely to be achieved under a fragmented hospital system which isolates the majority of patients (mental, geriatric, and subnormal) from the resources of the general hospital, or in a system of medical practice in which the hospital work of the general practitioner is separated (in community hospitals) from the work of the consultant.

QUALITY OF CARE

Since there is some confusion over terminology I should make it clear that I am using the term quality of care comprehensively to include (*a*) standard of care (how well we do what we do), (*b*) effectiveness of care (whether what we do is worth doing), and (*c*) efficiency of care (whether what we do makes better use of resources than the available alternatives).

Standard of care, as I conceive it, is concerned with appraisal of existing practices: by an individual, a profession, or an institution such as a hospital or health centre. It is not concerned with the usefulness of the services rendered nor with the cost/benefit issues which arise in relation to efficiency. Appraisal of standards may require assessment of the adequacy of facilities: buildings, equipment, etc., sometimes referred to as structure; or of the operation of services, sometimes described as process. Examination of standards has been relatively uncommon in Britain, largely because of conservative traditions, particularly the professional independence of the individual practitioner and consultant; it is more frequent in the United States where doctors are often willing to examine, and to have others examine critically, the standard of their work. Improvement in standards depends largely on the education and graduate training of doctors, and on the decision of professional organizations such as the Royal Colleges to take the subject very seriously.

I am using the terms effectiveness and efficiency essentially in the sense that Cochrane employed them, in reference not only to preventive and therapeutic measures such as vaccines, drugs, and surgery, but also to various features of the organization of care such as duration of stay in hospital and evaluation of home and hospital care. He emphasized particularly the use of randomized controlled trials in such assessments. All that need be added here is that the organization of the necessary investigations may be extremely complex, since they may require large-scale research involving several centres and continuing over a prolonged period. They may also be restricted by ethical considerations. One need think only of the problems arising currently in evaluation of screening for breast cancer to appreciate the difficulties. To those associated with assessment of effectiveness, appraisal of efficiency adds the further complication of estimation of *relative* benefits and costs of different procedures. However, I think it can be said without complacency that in examination of effectiveness at least, work in Britain compares not unfavourably with that in other countries. If we are cautious about evaluating how well we do what we do, we are at least fairly ready to consider whether it is worth doing.

However, the main point to be made about quality of care in the present context is a different one. We have overestimated the effectiveness of many procedures and services in current use, and indeed most have been adopted without adequate evaluation. It is important now, and with rising costs it will be imperative in future, to adopt a far more critical approach to appraisal of the various facets of quality: standard, effectiveness, and efficiency. Medicine must be prepared to face the tests which are inescapable in private enterprise and which it is almost unique among public activities in having evaded hitherto: Is our work well done? Is it worth doing? and Does it pay its way?

No one familiar with the problems associated with these assessments in medicine can be in any doubt about the difficulties, particularly in the case of procedures and services already in use. Once a procedure has come into general use it may be difficult, perhaps impossible to withdraw it after facilities have been provided, staff trained, and public expectations roused. However there is a point in time when a new measure is sufficiently promising to justify its introduction on a limited scale, and when it is not yet so widely used that there are ethical and other objections to investigation of its effectiveness. If this opportunity is missed it cannot easily be recreated, and it is for this reason that it is now difficult or impossible to assess the value of many procedures and services which have never been validated. There are, however, a few examples in recent years where a critical appraisal was made at the appropriate time, in clinical trials of vaccines and, more recently, in evaluation of screening procedures. There is little doubt that if this approach had not been adopted we should by now be committed to a breast cancer screening service of large cost, limited benefit, and unknown risks.

In the case of standards of care, given professional understanding and co-operation there should be no insuperable difficulty in improving existing procedures. But in consideration of effectiveness and efficiency attention should be focused particularly on new developments. Methods of investigation and treatment are likely to become more complex, costly, and, in some cases, hazardous than in the past. It should be the aim of policy to achieve control of such developments, and to ensure that no new procedure comes into general use until its benefits and costs have been estimated and its risks are known. These requirements apply to services in general; but they should be particularly stringent in the case of protective services such as screening. When people who believe themselves to be well are invited to submit to examination they should be assured not only that they may benefit but also that they are not being exposed to unknown risks.

(3) MEDICAL AND OTHER HEALTH WORKERS

In providing medical care the doctor has long relied on the co-operation of other workers, for example, in earlier centuries the apothecary who made up his prescriptions, and more recently the nurse who attends to his patients for much of the time when he is otherwise engaged. But in the twentieth century, and particularly the last few decades, there has been a large increase in the number of professionals and para-professionals who contribute to health care, and their relation to the doctor and to one another has become a major issue. Trade unionism, women's rights, professional prestige, and no doubt several other less readily specified influences have been at work, and the idea that the doctor is the natural leader of the health team, the person directly responsible to the patient for the effectiveness of his care in all circumstances, is no longer unchallenged.

This is not a new phenomenon; but it has become more significant. In Britain it has led to segregation from the medical services of social workers concerned with the sick, first in a separate department of local government and, since the reorganization of the NHS, under a separate authority. The environmental health officers of local authorities are no longer responsible to the medically qualified specialist who now serves as a consultant. And in the reorganized service, the objections of other health workers to medical dominance have been met by the concept of administration by consensus, a system of management designed to ensure that no one is managed. But in their relation to doctors the most important other professionals are undoubtedly nurses. In Britain they have so far accepted their traditional role with few complaints; however, in the United States nurses have asserted their independence by going their own way, and their training and role are now determined with little reference to medical tradition or opinion. In that country it might be said of doctors and nurses, as of two potential rivals, that they get on excellently because (in concepts and planning) they never meet.

The difficulties of professional relationships have existed for some time in the health field; but reaction to the doctor's position has been muted to some extent by the belief that his role is critical for the health of patients. Once it is realized that the determinants of health are largely outside the system, and that the main contribution required from personal health services is the care of the sick (using the term in its fullest sense), questions concerning medical dominance are likely to become even more insistent. Are the traditional roles of doctors and nurses appropriate in primary care, where the nurse appears to be capable of giving a service which in some countries the physician seems unable or unwilling to provide? Are responsibilities allocated sensibly in the acute ward, where it is the nurse rather than the doctor who is likely to be present at the time of serious emergencies? If the doctor is in charge in acute illness, does it follow that he should also be responsible in mental and chronic disease, where the patient's needs may be of an entirely different character? Is there a definable area of administration in which a medical qualification is essential, or should administrators, particularly senior ones, be selected as in other fields on the basis of personal gifts and experience which override technical qualifications?

These questions are not new; but they are given considerable urgency by a different reading of the determinants of health. If we accept that someone needs to be in charge of patient care and of administration of health services, it can no longer be assumed to be an automatic right of the doctor in all circumstances.

8

Medical education

In this chapter I shall suggest that the aims of medical education should be broader than they are at present; that it should be concerned with all the influences on health, non-personal as well as personal, and that in the field of patient care attention should be extended to all types of patients and all phases of illness.

A proposal of this kind is certain to provoke what many will regard as an insuperable objection. It will be said that patients come to doctors for assistance when they are unwell, and that the essential medical function is to meet this need; it is regrettable if this leads to some loss of interest in other influences on health and in the less active phases of care, but neither is exclusively a medical responsibility and this is a price which must be paid for concentration on the most important task: the diagnosis and treatment of disease in individual patients.

This is the logic which explains and is thought to justify the somewhat restricted aims of medical education. In challenging the conclusions two things must be shown: first, that 'other influences' are critical for health and require medical participation; and second, that when the diagnosis and treatment of disease is considered to be the essential medical function, many patients' needs are neglected.

OTHER INFLUENCES ON HEALTH

Their importance was discussed at some length in Chapter 6; the conclusions can be summarized by saying that health was transformed from the eighteenth century because of improved nutrition, better hygience, and contraception, and without a significant contribution from immunization and treatment before the twentieth century; and although the point is purely theoretical, it is unlikely that medical intervention would have been effective if the other advances had not occurred.

The role of medicine

In assessing the medical contribution which is needed a distinction must be made between environmental influences, which are essentially non-personal, and behavioural influences which are largely of a personal character.

Environmental influences. The grounds for retaining and extending the medical contribution to environmental medicine were outlined in Chapter 7. They are essentially the importance of the field, and the fact that although doctors often have little to contribute to the control of recognized hazards, identification of additional ones frequently results from observation of patients. In the case of hazards associated with investigation and treatment of disease, both recognition and control are almost inconceivable without medical participation.

The contribution of doctors to environmental medicine is of two kinds which have implications for medical education and postgraduate training. First, doctors in practice should be equipped to advise their patients about risks which may arise in relation to work, travel, domestic circumstances, and, occasionally, recreation. Second, medical specialists are needed who can contribute to investigation and control of hazards in all the main areas in which they arise: local, national, occupational, and medical. While some specialists may restrict their work to a particular area such as occupational health, it seems desirable that they should be trained basically in all aspects of environmental medicine, and that they should be identified professionally with other specialists who work in the same field.

Behavioural influences. In developed countries these are now the predominant determinants of health. In the past, modification of personal behaviour for health purposes was by the conventional forms of health education, a task assigned largely to non-medical people and one in which doctors as a whole took little interest. These arrangements had serious disadvantages: they separated assessment of unhealthy behaviour (undertaken mainly by research workers) from public communication (in the hands of professional educators); they placed the emphasis on an approach through posters, advertising, and public exhortation rather than through a more subtle and complex modification of ways of life; and they seemed to remove responsibility for health education from doctors in practice, who are often in the best position to influence the behaviour of their patients. More vigorous medical participation is needed, and it is unlikely to be achieved if the significance of personal behaviour, and the role of the doctor in relation to it, are not given sufficient attention in medical education.

AN EXTENDED CONCEPT OF PERSONAL CARE

In some respects more serious than the effect on other influences is the restricted concept of personal care which results from identification of diagnosis and treatment as the essential medical function. In hospital and consultant services it has led to the relative neglect of the majority of patients (the mentally ill, the subnormal, and the aged sick) who are not thought to provide scope for the investigative and therapeutic procedures which are the main concern of the acute hospitals. In Britain the deficiency is now well recognized; but the solution advocated is often a simple diversion of resources to the neglected areas, rather than a new approach to the whole relation between short, intermediate, and long-term care. It was suggested above (Chapter 7) that this is unlikely to be achieved by a hospital system which places different classes of patients in separate institutions.

Moreover the deficiencies of care are not restricted to those who are severely handicapped by mental illness, subnormality, or extreme age. Patients who are well cared for so long as they are under active investigation and treatment are often neglected during the later stages of their illness, particularly if these are protracted. Since the eighteenth century general hospitals have sought to avoid admission of those who are likely to outstay their welcome, and if after completion of active measures patients are neither dead nor sufficiently recovered to return home, they are, if possible, discharged to other institutions. In some countries the deficiencies go even further, and a patient with an incurable illness is no longer of much interest to the doctor who made the diagnosis. The lesson has not yet been learned everywhere that diagnosis of disease is of little value if it does not lead to effective treatment or care, and in general (there are some necessary

124

exceptions) care at different stages of an illness should not be divided between doctors and between institutions.

It will of course be said, and rightly, that in Britain these criticisms are more applicable to hospitals than to general practice, that many general practitioners provide prolonged care, including terminal care of patients in their own homes. At its best this service works reasonably well for domiciliary care; but it is sometimes not at its best, it is not available in hospitals, and in some countries it is not available at all. The general criticism remains valid; in medicine in the late twentieth century exaggeration of the contribution of investigation and treatment of disease leads to serious neglect of the substantial and continuing needs of many patients.

If interest is to be extended to non-personal influences on health and to all phases of care, changes will be needed in medical education. The conclusions must be considered in relation to selection of students, the medical curriculum, and the image of medicine projected at the teaching centre.

SELECTION OF STUDENTS

From time to time the question is asked whether the right people come into medicine; and although it is usually unanswered or inconclusively answered, perhaps it should be considered again whenever changes are proposed in the role and education of the doctor. My own experience of admission procedures, happily quite brief, was sufficient to convince me that Shaw's comment early in the century remains valid: 'Unless a man is led to medicine or surgery through a very exceptional technical aptitude, or because doctoring is a family tradition, or because he regards it unintelligently as a lucrative and gentlemanly profession, his motives in choosing the career of a healer are clearly generous.'[1] Perhaps today the exceptions should also include some who are influenced by examination success in the so-called basic sciences (physics, chemistry, biology, and mathematics) which many school and university teachers consider to be the best evidence of suitability for a career in medicine. (In the present context it is significant that medical schools often place more emphasis on

1. Preface to *The Doctor's Dilemma*.

physical than on biological science.) However there is no reason to doubt that most entrants to medical schools are strongly, and on the whole, generously motivated.

There is also no reason to question their intellectual abilities. Except in those unfortunate countries which have to accept all qualified students into the first year, medical schools everywhere have a high ratio of applicants to admission places. Since all university applications are assessed in much the same way, in Britain largely on results of 'O'- and 'A'-level examinations, students admitted to medical schools are probably at least as able as those entering other professions. Medicine cannot ask for more.

However students undoubtedly come into medicine with some very definite ideas about the career on which they are embarking and the training appropriate for it. Their ideas reflect the pre-dominant notions in society about the work of the doctor: that he is concerned with the diagnosis and treatment of disease in individual patients, that most patients are cured by treatment and that it is on medical intervention that health primarily depends. It is like a slap on the face for a student to be told at the outset of his training that at least on the second and third points these ideas need revision: that health is not determined mainly by medical intervention and that the needs of patients extend far beyond what can be achieved by investigation and active treatment.

When these concepts are widely known it is possible that they may have some influence on the decision of students to select medicine as a career; applicants should perhaps be drawn more frequently than at present from the two ends of a spectrum of interest from which recruitment is largely from the middle. An identikit of the contemporary medical student would be one who combines aptitude for physical and biological science with concern about the care of individual patients. But his interest in medical science is not such that he would wish to pursue it if it led away from personal care; and his concern about personal care is not strong enough for him to devote himself to it if divorced from investigation and active treatment. There is undoubtedly a larger place for people who are interested in the application of medical science through measures such as nutrition, environment, and population control, but who would not wish to undertake personal care; and for physicians who are selected primarily for their interest and concern for the welfare of patients, including those who are permanently handicapped. Such applicants are not easily recognized, but in the course of time, as the public image of medicine is modified, they may select themselves.

But although medicine would undoubtedly benefit from recruitment of some students who at present are more likely to find their way into engineering or social service, I do not think that the difficulty of training doctors to meet the needs of society arises because the wrong people are chosen. The students who enter medical schools are reasonably able and, in spite of some remarkable exceptions, generously motivated, and their idea of the determinants of health and of the doctor's role is only a reflection of the current views of society. The failure to enlarge the concept of the medical task (and the loss of motivation, where it occurs) are usually due to subsequent training, to what they hear and see during five years in a medical school and teaching hospital. The important influences are the medical curriculum and the image of medicine projected at the teaching hospital.

THE MEDICAL CURRICULUM

Although students are probably more influenced by the practice and research of the teaching centre than by what they hear in lectures and seminars, the medical curriculum is important, not least as an indication of the subjects and methods which are considered relevant to the education of a doctor. While there is some variation from school to school, and considerable variation from country to country, there is no serious dispute about the basic concepts; medicine is thought to be concerned with intervention in disease processes, mainly by investigation and treatment of established disease, but also by immunization against infections and, to a limited extent, by early recognition of disease through screening. Since the intervention is by physical, chemical, and biological methods it is not surprising that the basic sciences are considered to be physics, chemistry, and biology; that medical education begins with study of the structure and function of the body (anatomy, physiology, and biochemistry); that it continues with examination of disease processes (pathology and microbiology); and that it ends with clinical instruction on selected patients of the types seen in a teaching hospital.

The limitations of this approach were discussed in Chapter 2. The preoccupation with disease mechanisms leads away from consideration of the underlying causes of disease whose control is the essential basis of improvement in health. More surprisingly, considering that interest is focused on the sick patient, the approach also results in failure to assess critically the effectiveness of medical intervention, and to consider adequately patients' needs which are additional to investigation and active treatment.

The following are among changes needed in medical education to enlarge the concepts of health and disease and the role of medicine arising from them.

1. At the outset it should be recognized that the most fundamental question in medicine is why disease occurs rather than how it operates after it has occurred; that is to say, conceptually the origins of disease should take precedence over the nature of disease process. The starting-point in education should therefore be the distinction between diseases established irreversibly at fertilization and those which are not, and the instruction should be concerned with genes and chromosomes, with the prenatal environment and with the wide range of post-natal influences, both physical and mental. It would be desirable to consider also the disease experience of early man and of other animals in their natural habitats. Considerable attention should be given to matters which have been examined in a very preliminary way in this book: the nature of the influences which have brought about the transformation in human health, and of those which may be expected to be effective in dealing with the residual health problems of developed countries.

These are not matters to be dealt with and dismissed in a series of lectures, although no doubt there is a place for a course or courses related to them. The conclusion that human health is determined by the conditions under which disease occurs is one which should influence all stages of teaching. In the early years it should enlarge the mechanistic approach of the pre-clinical departments; in the intermediate period it should complement the teaching of the pathological sciences; and in clinical medicine it should lead to a more searching discussion of disease origins in relation to individual patients.

2. In clinical teaching discussion is focused on investigation, diagnosis, pathogenesis, clinical manifestations, and treatment of disease. Questions which usually receive insufficient attention are: Why is the patient ill? How effective is the treatment and what risks are associated with it? What advice and care are needed, by the patient or his relatives after completion of active measures?

The attention given to disease origins varies from one field of medicine to another and from consultant to consultant within the same field. In general, this subject is considered more fully by physicians than by surgeons and, understandably, by surgeons concerned with cold surgery than by those dealing mainly with acute cases. Moreover the time devoted to the origins of disease is increasing, if slowly, and some teachers review comprehensively what is known about aetiology. Nevertheless, this subject does not have the central place in clinical teaching that its importance merits; and understandably, since the essential tasks of the doctor are considered to be diagnosis and treatment. In these circumstances it is disease mechanisms rather than disease origins which provide the basis for discussion—How does the disease operate, so that we may intervene? rather than—What are the conditions which lead to it, so that we may remove them? It is surely unnecessary to add that in emphasizing the importance of the second question one is not suggesting that the first should be neglected. But the origin of disease deserves consideration even where it is unknown, for example in relation to many problems unresolved at the present time: multiple sclerosis, diabetes, Parkinsonism, schizophrenia, varicose veins, etc., as well as such ill-defined conditions as backache and the multiple forms of rheumatism. The purpose of raising these uncomfortable issues is twofold: to make doctors in practice acutely aware of the extent and limitations of knowledge of the causes (as well as the mechanisms) of disease; and to lead future research workers to reflect on the outstanding problems on the basis of something more than the conventional mechanistic approach.

3. The question concerning the effectiveness and risks of intervention can be raised with advantage on almost every patient. Again it must be said that some teachers do consider it, and a few regard it as of outstanding importance; but in general, the value and hazards of investigation and treatment are not discussed critically, and doctors complete their education with only vague ideas about the credentials of many of the procedures they are expected to apply. The basic difficulty is of course, as Cochrane has emphasized,[1] that the effectiveness of most clinical procedures has never been adequately assessed; but what is not known, as well as what is known, should be made explicit in clinical teaching. To give one example: since only a minority of practising doctors are surgeons (and they train for the specialty as graduates), and a majority have to give advice from time to time about the value of surgical procedures, consideration of outcome in library, ward rounds, and seminars is more relevant to their needs than time spent in operating theatres.

4. Probably the most serious deficiency in clinical teaching is in respect of the care needed by patients after completion of investigation and treatment, and by those, the majority of all hospital patients, who are not considered to provide scope for active measures and so are never seen in teaching hospitals. This deficiency is attributable more to the limited range of work of the teaching hospital (discussed below) than to clinical teaching. Nevertheless the emphasis on investigation and acute care inevitably gives students the impression that the later needs of patients, less dramatic but no less important, are a secondary consideration which can often be left to someone else. It leads to the remarkable notions that the diagnosis of a disease which cannot be treated is an end in itself, and that treatment of acute illness in an elderly person can be divorced from rehabilitative measures and terminal care.

Any comment on the deficiencies of medical education is open to the criticism that it is not equally true of all subjects and of all teachers. And of course, it is not; there are some who consider

1. Cochrane, A. L., *Effectiveness and Efficiency*, Rock Carling Monograph, 1971 (Nuffield Provincial Hospitals Trust, 1972).

carefully the origins of disease and the effectiveness and hazards of treatment, although they must find it almost impossible to deal convincingly with the later phases of care or with permanently handicapped people within the confines of a teaching hospital. In view of this difficulty most medical schools have introduced instruction in general practice, which extends students' experience to domiciliary care and, to a limited extent, to the later stages of illness. Nevertheless the criticisms of medical education outlined above remain valid; being based on a mechanistic concept of disease and of medical intervention, it begins with consideration of the structure and function of the body, continues with discussion of disease processes and ends with clinical experience of selected hospital patients. In such circumstances it is very difficult to convey that medicine has a vital contribution to the non-personal and behavioural influences which are the main determinants of ill health, and that the care of patients who are permanently handicapped or in terminal illness is as much a part of the medical responsibility as investigation and treatment of acute disease.

5. It was suggested above that there is need for medical specialists who devote themselves wholly to environmental medicine. Such specialists cannot be expected to emerge unless the subject is presented adequately when they are undergraduates. A recent survey of medical schools in the United Kingdom showed that only 15 of 25 schools gave any formal instruction in occupational health: the part of the field that has had most attention in medical education; and the time allowed was generally small: less than six hours in 8 of the 15 schools which included some teaching.

THE IMAGE OF MEDICINE PROJECTED AT THE TEACHING
CENTRE

But the really potent influence on students, and through them on the subsequent operation of health services, is neither the selection procedures of medical schools nor the design of medical curricula; it is the image of medicine which emerges from the range of activities and interests of the teaching centre.

Medical education

It is not difficult to understand how the restriction of the work of teaching hospitals came about; it resulted from grafting the concept of scientific medicine on to the tradition of the voluntary hospitals.

From the time of their rebirth under secular auspices in the eighteenth century the large voluntary hospitals attempted to limit their work to short-term remediable cases which were of greatest interest to the medical staff and were said to make the best use of their resources. Thus they excluded the majority of patients who had to be cared for in separate voluntary hospitals (for example, for women and children) or in public institutions (for the infectious, the mentally ill, and the destitute).

It is important to recognize that the work of voluntary hospitals was not designed to meet the needs of medical education; on the contrary, medical education had to conform to the established traditions of the hospitals. In Britain at the end of the eighteenth century the training of doctors was still mainly in private profit-making schools and there were nineteen different corporations with the power to examine and license medical practitioners. Only three London hospitals (St Bartholomew's, the United Hospitals (St Thomas's and Guy's), and the London) had medical schools attached to them. The association between medical education and voluntary hospitals did not develop rapidly until the nineteenth century, when the College of Surgeons and the Society of Apothecaries included hospital work among requirements from candidates for their examinations. By this time the lines of interest of some of the major hospitals had been drawn for more than a hundred years.

Moreover there was no disposition on the part of teachers to challenge the limited spectrum of interests at the hospitals, since they were themselves the consultants, or the heirs of the consultants, who had been largely responsible for restricting their work. Indeed the opportunity to have students who would later refer patients was one of the attractions of hospital appointments, and it would have been surprising indeed if the teaching commitment had led consultants to challenge the premises on which their own work was based. It has scarcely done so a hundred and fifty years later when there is less excuse for failure to recognize the limitations of the earlier tradition.

Eventually, of course, some hospitals were founded as teaching hospitals (University College Hospital, for example, in 1828). But by this time the idea of the acute general hospital as the focus of medical education was deeply rooted, and the role of the new hospitals established for teaching did not differ significantly from that of the existing hospitals to which teaching responsibilities were added later. In this way medical education became based on institutions which attempted to exclude (among other patients) the destitute and the infectious, at a time when poverty was widespread and infection the predominant cause of death. Preoccupied with his own interests, the consultant teacher had apparently not noticed that he had removed from the attention of the student the most formidable medical problems of his day. In doing so he also determined the direction of medical education and the scope of the work of the teaching centre for more than a century.

The exclusive character of the work of the teaching centre was further accentuated by the trend towards scientific medicine on which the Flexner Report had so great an influence. Flexner suggested that 'medical education must be conceived as primarily the effort to train students in the intellectual technique of inductive science', a view which would be widely endorsed in academic circles today. He recognized that 'education in science is somewhat different from the acquisition of information and the control of mechanism; it concerns itself fundamentally with habituation to method'. In a very significant passage he went on to say: 'Knowledge is indeed necessary, inasmuch as scientific method does not operate in a vacuum. A selection must therefore be made, and, unless the teacher is perverse, it will be made with general, *though by no means uniform*, reference to the objects of professional train' (italics inserted).

These ideas have influenced the thinking of a generation. Whether justly or not, they have been interpreted to strengthen the case for selectiveness. If a student is taught to think clearly and critically, if he learns (for example) to understand the inflammatory process, to examine the central nervous system, and to interpret an electrocardiograph and X-ray, he can apply his knowledge and methods in the very varied circumstances in which he may find himself after qualification, and for which in any case it would be impossible for medical education to prepare him in detail. From this it is concluded that the exhibition of a wide range of patients and services to students is a secondary consideration; indeed experience of the scientific method can be acquired more readily from a small number of patients carefully selected and fully investigated. And if some or all of these patients are the focus of the research interests of the clinical teacher, this can only make the instruction more stimulating and effective than otherwise it would be.

The effects of the traditions of the teaching hospitals on medical education have been profound. A medical service can be no more enlightened than the minds of the doctors who provide it, and the intellectual shutters are never again so widely open as during the period of training. Inevitably students acquire their concept of practice from the example provided by their teachers, and they leave the hospital aspiring to engage in the work they saw when training.

It is for this reason that the isolation of teaching from some of the major health problems is so serious. A centre which excludes the mentally ill, the subnormal, and many of the aged sick cannot be expected to provide doctors who will care for them; and even the token admission of a few of these patients does not convey the idea that these are the largest and most formidable problems by which medicine is now confronted. It is therefore not possible to staff the major services unless the full range of problems and methods is displayed at the teaching centre where the work and interests of the future doctor are determined.

The effects of the restrictions are even more grotesque in developing countries, where the western model has been adopted with little modification, and without regard for the vastly different problems and resources. Teaching hospitals are usually remote from the rural areas where most people live and the health needs are greatest. Indeed it is one of the anomalies of medical education that, with its focus on disease mechanisms rather than disease problems, it aspires to a concept of practice which is uniform and presupposes the existence of selected patients and the availability of unlimited resources.

The role of medicine

I have discussed elsewhere the changes needed to correct the deficiencies.[1] Ideally the teaching centre should accept responsibility for all medical services for the population of a defined area, or where this is not possible, for all hospital services and a close association with domiciliary and other health and related social services.

MEDICAL AND OTHER HEALTH WORKERS

There is a further point which concerns the relation between the trainings of medical and other health workers. It is perhaps not too fanciful to imagine that in this context history might be divided into three periods: the first, ending in 1858, when major issues divided the various classes of medical workers: physicians, surgeons, and apothecaries; the second, from the passing of the First Medical Act (in 1858) to the present day, when doctors were a uniform profession, dominant in the health scene and with no major problems in their relation to one another or to other workers; and a third period which we have now entered, when important issues arise concerning the respective roles of medicine and other health professions. It is significant that in the present period the concept of a uniform medical profession is also being eroded, by the introduction (particularly in the United States) of a substantial element of elective work in medical education. Doctors are no longer identical at the time they take their medical qualification, but have already established in a preliminary way their roles as specialists. It is difficult to be confident about the long term effects of this trend, for good or ill. But what should be noted is that the relation of doctors to nurses, social workers, hygienists, indeed to all the major groups in the health field, becomes very much an open question when the identity of the physician himself is no longer so clearly defined.

1. McKeown, T., *Medicine in Modern Society* (London: George Allen and Unwin Ltd, 1965), pp. 213-21.

9

Medical research

In his poem, based on the myth of Leda and the Swan, Yeats asked whether the girl, seduced by the transformed God, 'put on his knowledge with his power'.[1] The same question when inverted might be asked about medicine today: Did it put on its power with its knowledge? However it is one of the charms of the fable that it is open to more than one interpretation, and I must avoid misunderstanding by stating the issue more precisely: Are the improvements in health with which medicine is commonly credited determined essentially by medical science, or are they due largely to fortuitous changes in which biomedical research has played little part?

Most scientists, certainly most medical scientists, are in no doubt about the answer. Since the eighteenth century health has been transformed; since the nineteenth century medical knowledge has greatly increased; and in the twentieth century there have been remarkable advances in technology. These events are assumed to be causally related, the improvement in health being attributed to the growth of knowledge, and the new knowledge, essentially, to medical research. From this interpretation of the past hopes are projected into the future; what science is believed to have done is thought to give grounds for confidence in what science can be expected to do. Yesterday the decline of the infections, tomorrow control of cancer and mental illness. Indeed as Burnet has reminded us, medical research workers hold a unique place among scientists largely because their work is believed to contribute powerfully to the saving of human life.[2]

Any questioning of these views can be counted on to provoke an immediate and sharp response. In his book, *Genes, Dreams and*

1.   'So mastered by the brute blood of the air,
       Did she put on his knowledge with his power?'
   2. Burnet, Sir Macfarlane, *Genes, Dreams and Realities* (Aylesbury, Bucks: Medical and Technical Publishing Co. Ltd, 1971), p. 226.

Realities, Burnet concluded that 'the contribution of laboratory science has virtually come to an end' and 'almost none of modern basic research in the medical sciences has any direct bearing on the prevention of disease or on the improvement of medical care'.[1] One reviewer reacted to these heresies like a devout clergyman who has heard his bishop express doubts about the divinity of Jesus Christ. Burnet was accused not merely of scientific error, but even more seriously, of lacking faith in the potential of science.

And finally the contribution to medicine that can be expected from laboratory research as a whole. The major medical problems now facing advanced societies are indeed difficult ones; no one expects rapid or dramatic solutions (although they may turn up, as they have so often done before, in the most unexpected ways). But one can be sure of one thing; solutions will not come without laboratory research. If society wants solutions to current medical problems (and it does), then it is laboratory research that it must support. There are no alternatives.[2]

It is perhaps not stretching the clerical analogy too far to suggest that this passage is concerned with faith as well as fact: 'Believe or ye are lost', and in the last despairing sentence, 'Believe and ye may still be lost'.

But it would be wrong to imply that medical scientists' estimate of the contribution of their work is attributable largely to emotion; many believe that they have assessed health problems objectively when they say that the ability to prevent sickness and premature death is based on knowledge derived from laboratory research, often of the pure variety. When considering the contribution of technology to medicine Thomas wrote: 'If I were a policy-maker, interested in saving money for health care over the long haul, I would regard it as an act of high prudence to give high priority to a lot more basic research in biologic science.'[3] And in a discussion of pure and applied research Medawar concluded: 'We encourage pure research in these situations because we know no other way to go about it. If we knew of a direct

1. Burnet, op. cit., p. 218.
2. Harris, Henry, *British Medical Journal,* 3 (1971), p. 712.
3. Thomas, L., *The Lives of a Cell* (Toronto, New York, London: Bantam Books, Inc., 1975), p. 41.

pathway leading to the solution of the clinical problem of rheumatoid arthritis, can anyone seriously believe that we should not take it?'[1]

I believe that the thinking of those who take this view of the contribution of medical research is influenced by the Cartesian model; in concluding that improvements in health are derived from understanding of the structure and function of the body and of the disease processes that affect it they are carrying over to living things principles which have been applied successfully to inanimate matter. But they would long since have rejected this model if it were thought to be seriously inconsistent with experience. The fact that they have not done so indicates that they believe the decline of infectious disease, the main reason for the improvement in health, was due essentially to the increased knowledge provided by medical science. To evaluate this conclusion we must examine closely the contribution of science and technology to the main influences, nutritional, environmental, behavioural, and medical, which were responsible for the reduction of infectious deaths.

SCIENCE, TECHNOLOGY, AND HEALTH

In assessing the impact of science and technology it will be desirable to distinguish clearly between the following:

1. Measures which, although scientific in character, owed little if anything to professional science. I am thinking, for example, of manuring of land by farmers and limitation of family size by parents.

2. Measures which relied on investigations of a relatively simple epidemiological kind. I refer to the observations on living conditions and health which led to the introduction of environmental improvements before the nature of infectious disease was understood.

3. Non-medical science and technology which extended the simple measures referred to under 1: for example, chemical fertilizers, insecticides, and herbicides in agriculture, and engineering technology which contributed to control of the environment.

1. Medawar, P. B., *The Art of the Soluble* (Great Britain: Pelican Books, 1969), p. 137.

4. Biomedical research which extended non-personal measures. Perhaps the best example is the understanding of the nature of infectious disease which led to improvements in hygiene of water and food.

5. Biomedical research which resulted in immunization and treatment.

In the present context it will be particularly interesting to distinguish the contribution of medical science (4 and 5) from that of other influences (1, 2, and 3); and within medical science, to see the extent to which its impact was through personal measures (immunization and therapy) as distinct from non-personal measures such as hygiene and better food. For the application of the Cartesian model to the problems of human health might be interpreted in either of two ways. It might be taken to mean that health depended on understanding of the body and disease processes, that is on the significance of both 4 and 5. Or, on a stricter interpretation of the concept of the body as a machine, it might be interpreted to mean that health was determined by the personal measures of immunization and therapy referred to under 5.

I shall consider briefly the nature of the more important developments before commenting on their scientific character.

NUTRITION

The improvement in nutrition was due initially to advances in agriculture which spread throughout the western world from about the end of the seventeenth century. The following developments were particularly important to the production and distribution of food.

(*a*) Improvement in organization, particularly enclosure of land which encouraged more efficient farming.

(*b*) Advances in farming practice, which included conservation of fertility, crop rotation, seed production, winter feeding, minor improvements in farm implements and, notably, the introduction of root crops, particularly the potato and, in warm climates, maize.

(*c*) Improvements in transport, initially by navigable rivers and roads but later by canals.

These were the critical advances in the eighteenth and nineteenth centuries, and they led to a large increase in food production. Hutchinson attached particular importance to the restoration of fertility through manuring,[1] and Langer assembled impressive evidence for the significance of root crops, introduced from the New World in the seventeenth century.[2] Whatever the relative importance of the different advances there is no doubt that they resulted from more intensive and systematic use of traditional farming methods rather than the introduction of new ones. From the second half of the nineteenth century, however, agricultural output was increased further by mechanization, chemical fertilizers and later, insecticides and herbicides.

HYGIENE

The question whether the environmental measures developed in the nineteenth century were intially of a scientific kind is an intriguing one. It might be argued that they were not, on the grounds that Chadwick, the most effective advocate of reform, did not accept the explanation for their success suggested by the work of Pasteur: that micro-organisms were the cause of infectious diseases. However the ideas which led Chadwick and his colleagues to the conclusion that the environment was an important source of illness had been evolving over more than a century. As early as 1719, when plague appeared again in southern Europe, Richard Meade suggested not only more stringent application of traditional measures (isolation and quarantine) but also much wider improvements in the community: better housing, cleanliness, ventilation, disinfection, and control of nuisances. A little later there were notable investigations of the association between living conditions and disease, by Pringle in the army, Lind in the navy, and Howard in his poignant journey through English prisons in the winter of 1773. Two practical demonstrations of the feasibility of control of disease by environmental measures were the observations that scurvy could be prevented by eating fresh fruit, and that the colic which was endemic in Devon was

1. Hutchinson, J., 'Land and human populations', *The Advancement of Science*, **23** (1966), 241.
2. Langer, W. L., 'American foods and Europe's population growth, 1750–1850', *Journal of Social History*, Winter Number (1975), p. 51.

attributable to lead poisoning. But perhaps the most significant inquiry was largely the work of Chadwick himself, who published in 1842 his *Report on the Sanitary Conditions of the Labouring Population of Great Britain.* This document examined the relation between environmental conditions and ill-health. By later standards much of the evidence was deficient; nevertheless it was essentially of an epidemiological kind which today, in spite of methodological reservations, we should unhesitatingly regard as scientific.

The effectiveness of hygienic measures was greatly extended from the time when Pasteur established the bacterial origin of infectious diseases. Microbiology was of course the source of preventive and therapeutic measures applied to the individual; but it also contributed powerfully to advances in hygiene which were even more important, for example by showing how infection is spread, and making it possible to identify specific diseases, including their unsuspected presence in 'carriers'.

REPRODUCTIVE BEHAVIOUR

There were no specific biological or other scientific developments behind the modification of reproductive behaviour which led to the decline of the birth-rate. It might, perhaps, be said that the work of Malthus and, less directly, of Darwin had drawn attention to the importance of control of numbers; but by 1870 when the birth-rate began to decline, this knowledge can have reached only a small and selected segment of the population. Moreover, in France the fall of the birth-rate began much earlier, and indeed was already evident at the end of the eighteenth century when Malthus was writing. It therefore seems reasonable to conclude that in the beginning the limitation of numbers was due, not to any identifiable scientific advance, but to the fact that large numbers of people had reached the conclusion that the lives of their families would be improved if they restricted the number of children. I shall not attempt to speculate on whether this simple observation was in some sense scientific; what is not in doubt is that methods of control of reproduction were later extended by science, although their contribution in practice is still something of an open question.

IMMUNIZATION AND THERAPY

Many medical scientists believe that the control of bacterial infections is based on knowledge of infectious diseases derived from basic research and applied largely, although by no means exclusively, through immunization and therapy. In Chapter 6 I arrived at quite a different conclusion: that these measures 'had little effect on the death rate before 1935 and since that time have been less important than other influences?' The grounds for this conclusion were discussed earlier and here it will be necessary only to summarize the evidence for England and Wales. This can be done by considering briefly some of the infections in which immunization and therapy are generally considered important.

Tuberculosis. BCG vaccination had little or no influence on the decline of mortality. Streptomycin reduced mortality by about half from the time when it was introduced (1947) but over the whole period since cause of death was first registered its contribution to the reduction of deaths was about 3 per cent.

Pneumonia. Chemotherapy had a moderate effect on mortality at ages 0–14 and 45–64, but the effect on deaths at all ages was not large and was certainly not the main reason for the continued decline of the death-rate which was well established from the beginning of the century.

Diphtheria. Antitoxin is believed to have lowered the case fatality rate from the late nineteenth century; but more impressive was the rapid fall of mortality from about the time when national immunization was introduced (1941).

Measles and whooping cough. Mortality from both diseases fell to a low level without effective immunization or treatment. The usefulness of immunization is now being assessed by the effect on morbidity; the results so far are not very impressive.

Poliomyelitis. This disease has been almost eliminated from countries which have effective vaccination programmes. However, although it leads to conspicuous disabilities, poliomyelitis was not a common infection. In 1947 (before the introduction of vaccination) there were 33 deaths from the disease per million children under 15, compared with 99 for whooping cough and 69 from measles. In 1871–80, before the reduction of mortality began, the last two diseases were responsible for 1,415 and 1,038 deaths (per million under 15) and respiratory tuberculosis for 2,126 per million at all ages.

Smallpox. The decline of deaths is believed to be due mainly to vaccination. However, vaccination was made compulsory only in the mid nineteenth century (it was not enforced until 1871) and since that time smallpox has been associated with 1·6 per cent of the reduction of the death-rate from all causes.

Syphilis. This disease was responsible for 0·3 per cent of the decrease of mortality from the mid nineteenth century to 1971. The number of deaths fell rapidly from 1916, when salvarsan was made generally available, and was quite low in 1945 when penicillin largely replaced the arsenical preparations.

Tetanus. Mortality fell from 7 per million before the First World War to below 0·5 per million today. Both passive and active immunization are believed to have contributed to the decline but they were not the only, or necessarily, the most important influences.

The conclusion to be drawn from this assessment is not that immunization or treatment were of no value; on the contrary, they were probably effective in all the diseases listed above. But their impact on mortality and associated morbidity was small in relation to that of other influences. Diphtheria was the only *common* infection in which a specific measure, immunization, may have been the main reason for its decline; in the other common ones (tuberculosis, pneumonia, measles, whooping cough (and scarlet fever might be added)) mortality had fallen to a relatively low level before effective medical intervention was possible. The other diseases referred to above (smallpox, syphilis, poliomyelitis, and tetanus) in which specific measures are generally regarded as the main reason for their decline, taken singly or collectively made only a small contribution to the total reduction of infectious deaths.

This appraisal suggests that the modern improvement in health was initiated and carried quite a long way with little contribution from science and technology, except for the epidemiological investigations of environmental conditions in the eighteenth and early nineteenth centuries. This was true of the increase in food production, the beginning of hygienic measures and control of numbers. These advances resulted from simple but fundamental observations on everyday life: conservation of fertility increased agricultural output, hygienic measures prevented infectious diseases, and limitation of the number of births improved the conditions of life for parents and their children.

However, from the second half of the nineteenth century the original steps were extended by scientific developments of a non-personal kind (3 and 4 above). Some of these (for example chemical fertilizers and mechanization in agriculture, technology in distribution of water, and refrigeration in transportation of food) owed little or nothing to biomedical science and would have been introduced even if no health grounds were involved. But for extension and refinement of methods of preventing the spread of infectious diseases we are indebted to medical science and particularly to laboratory research.

Medical measures (immunization or therapy) began to influence the trend of mortality from one or two diseases (smallpox and syphilis) in the late nineteenth and early twentieth centuries; but they had no effect on deaths from the common infections before the introduction of sulphonamides and antibiotics in the 1930s, and even since that time, except in the case of tuberculosis they have been less important than other influences.

Since this interpretation of the contribution of science in the past has a considerable bearing on the approach to research in the future, it is important to consider a possible ground for reservation. Is it conceivable that things might have been quite different, that it was an accident of history that agricultural and other advances preceded effective medical intervention, and had the latter been available earlier its impact on mortality would have been more impressive? The effect of immunization and therapy on a population which is underfed and heavily exposed to infection is something of an open question; so far as it goes, experience of the World Health Organization in developing countries suggests that it is questionable whether infectious disease can be controlled by vaccination in a malnourished population. But if there is doubt about the effectiveness of medical measures in the absence of advances in nutrition and hygiene, there is none about the effectiveness of advances in nutrition and hygiene in the absence of medical measures. Experience of the last two centuries indicates that infectious deaths fell to a small fraction of their earlier level without medical intervention, and suggests that had none been available they would have continued to decline, if not quite so rapidly in some diseases.

BIOMEDICAL RESEARCH

Those who look mainly to laboratory research for the solution of current health problems do so under some misapprehensions about its achievements in the past. They underestimate the part that has been played by a rising standard of living and the accompanying advance in literacy, and they overestimate the contribution of laboratory medicine, particularly as applied through immunization and therapy. However they are not mistaken in regarding as important the increased understanding of disease processes which resulted from biomedical science, taking that term to include both laboratory and epidemiological research.

The tendency to overestimate the significance of laboratory investigation is well illustrated by a recent assessment of the contribution of basic and applied research to 'lifesaving advances' in cardiovascular and pulmonary diseases.[1] The advances examined were open-heart surgery, blood vessel surgery, treatment of hypertension, management of coronary artery disease, prevention of poliomyelitis, chemotherapy of tuberculosis and acute rheumatic

1. Comroe (Jr), J. H., and Dripps, R. D., 'Scientific basis for the support of biomedical science', *Science*, 192 (1976), 105.

fever, cardiac resuscitation and cardiac pacemakers, oral diuretics (for treatment of high blood pressure or of congestive heart failure), intensive care units, and new diagnostic methods. The authors were able to show that these advances relied largely on work which 'was not clinically oriented at the time it was done', and they concluded 'that a generous portion of the nation's biomedical research dollars should be used to identify and then to provide long-term support for creative scientists whose main goal is to learn how living organisms function, without regard to the immediate relation of their research to specific human diseases'.

In the present context what is remarkable is not the suggestion that fundamental research is indispensible, but the selection of advances on which this conclusion is based. Of the ten listed above, one is concerned with methods, and is therefore only a means to a therapeutic end. Two others refer to a large contribution to a relatively small problem (prevention of poliomyelitis) or to small contributions to large problems (chemotherapy of tuberculosis and acute rheumatic fever). The rest are all examples of what Thomas describes as 'halfway technology . . . the kinds of things that must be done after the fact, in efforts to compensate for the incapacitating effects of certain diseases whose course one is unable to do very much about'.[1] Such measures may prolong life for a few years; but they do not prevent the diseases, nor do they restore the patient to a life of normal duration and quality.

The distinction between prolonging life for a limited period and the solution of a major disease problem may also be illustrated by reference to diabetes. The discovery of insulin is regarded as one of the landmarks in the history of medical research and it is sometimes said that 'insulin enables diabetics to live as long as other persons and to have as many children'.[2] Certainly it is true that insulin has prolonged many lives; nevertheless in England and Wales diabetes was given as the primary cause of 5,127 deaths (nearly 1 per cent of all deaths) in 1973, and it must also have been entered as a secondary cause in many more. And while diabetics

1. Thomas, L., *The Lives of a Cell* (Toronto, New York, London: Bantam Books, Inc., 1975), p. 37.
2. Dubos, R., *Man, Medicine and Environment* (London: Pall Mall Press, 1968), p. 85.

who would formerly have been sterile now have normal children, the pregnancy of a diabetic woman is still a source of anxiety; even in the best hospitals, perinatal mortality is close to 10 per cent, about five times the rate in non-diabetic mothers.[1] It is also doubtful whether treatment can control the secondary complications of the disease: for example cataract, neuropathy, and vascular disease.[2] Clearly, although the multiple problems which arise from diabetes have been greatly alleviated by insulin, they have by no means been solved.

In making our cheerful assessments of the results of research whose goal 'is to learn how living organisms function', we have been looking through a lens of high power at a small segment of a large field. Within that segment the advances from laboratory science have of course been very valuable; but over the whole range of disease problems their contribution was limited, and it would have been seen to be limited if human health had not been transformed in the same period by other influences. The key to the main direction of medical research in future lies in close appraisal of these influences.

In Chapter 6 it was concluded that in order of importance the determinants of health were nutritional, environmental, and behavioural in the past, and will probably be behavioural, environmental, and nutritional in the future, at least in developed countries. The theoretical grounds for their effectiveness were outlined in Chapter 2. During his evolution man, like other living things, was exposed to rigorous natural selection which restricted disease determined irreversibly at fertilization to a low frequency. Most diseases and disabilities are therefore due to environmental influences operating on variable genetic material, and the solution of disease problems depends essentially on the removal or modification of the deleterious agents.

On this interpretation of common diseases, a full understanding of disease processes is often unnecessary for their control. The decline of infectious deaths preceded by more than a hundred

1. Leading article, *British Medical Journal*, **2** (1976), 267.
2. Butterfield, W. J. H., 'Diabetes mellitus', in *Screening in Medical Care* (London, New York, Toronto: Oxford University Press for the Nuffield Provincial Hospitals Trust, 1968), p. 76.

years the discovery of micro-organisms; withdrawal of thalidomide and avoidance of exposure to rubella in pregnancy prevented
the associated malformations without knowledge of teratogenesis;
and cessation of smoking by doctors lowered the incidence of
cancer of the lung in spite of very incomplete information about
the natural history of the disease and the mechanism of carcino-
genesis.

The grounds for reservations concerning the conventional
view of health problems—that their solution requires knowledge
of disease acquired by laboratory research and applied mainly
through medical intervention—are therefore both pragmatic and
conceptual. This explanation is not in accord with past experience;
nor is it consistent with interpretation of the origin of disease.

The conclusion that a detailed knowledge of mechanisms is
often not essential for the solution of biological problems is confirmed by experience of everyday life. One of the best sires at stud
is a horse called *Vaguely Noble*, whose reputation is based on the
observations that he was himself a great racehorse and that he has
already sired some very fast offspring, including *Pawneese* (the
leading 3-year-old in Europe, unbeaten to 1976) and the great
French filly, *Dahlia*. This success owes nothing to unravelling of
the genetic code or even to Mendelism or Darwinism, but is based
on breeding practices that have been in use since plants and animals
were first domesticated ten thousand years ago. . . . Some of the
finest wines ever made, for example La Tâche, La Romanée, and
La Romanée-Conti, are produced without assistance from laboratory science in a few acres of Burgundy, by combining knowledge
of soil, sun, wind, and rain, with traditions of wine-making that
have been perfected with pride and affection, and passed from
father to son and from nobleman to peasant for generations. Does
anyone imagine that within the foreseeable future faster racehorses
could be bred by modifications of gene structure, or that wines of
equal or greater subtlety could be manufactured by substituting
chemical and biological methods for the traditional viniculture?

The problems which would arise in dealing with common
diseases by intervention at the molecular or cellular level are no
less formidable. Indeed since piano playing, to take another
example, involves only two variables, interval and pressure,

technically speaking the replacement of Kempff's Beethoven and Rubenstein's Chopin by mechanically produced sound would be hardly more than a five-finger exercise, by comparison with the difficulties of preventing mental subnormality, cancer, or heart disease by control of genes.

AN ALTERNATIVE APPROACH

Fortunately there are other approaches to the solution of health problems; indeed some have already been used extensively, although with the focus on biomedical research of a laboratory type this is often overlooked. However, I should make it clear that I am not presuming to outline a blueprint for medical research; I shall attempt only to indicate some directions which follow from the conclusion that for improvements in health we must rely largely in future, as in the past, on modification of environmental (ie non-genetic) influences.

HEALTH INTELLIGENCE

Perhaps the first requirement is for a systematic appraisal of problems against the background of conclusions concerning the determinants of health. So long as it was thought that control of disease depended primarily on the study of disease processes ('the milieu interieur'), it is understandable that there was little interest in external influences. We now need a close examination of the size, character, and feasibility of control of disease problems in the light of a classification of the type proposed at the end of Chapter 2. In particular we should identify conditions determined at fertilization, and among conditions not so determined, distinguish congenital abnormalities from those in which the deleterious influences are post-natal. Attempts should also be made to exploit national and other sources in investigating the nature of environmental influences and the extent of their effects. It is surely remarkable that medical people have left to historians the task of assessing the reasons for the decline of mortality in the past, and, to take only one example, that they have not considered carefully whether smoking accounts largely for the difference in expectation of life between men and women.

I conclude that any organization concerned with the support of medical research should devote a significant part of its attention to health intelligence.

CONGENITAL ABNORMALITIES

This term is taken to comprise not only physical malformations but also disturbances of function, such as mental subnormality, which are present at birth. One of the most significant conclusions in Chapter 2 was that while few of these congenital conditions are determined irreversibly at fertilization, most are unlikely to be controlled either by removal of adverse influences during pregnancy or by treatment after birth. The possibilities which remain are prevention of conception or elimination by abortion.

On present knowledge we have no grounds for optimism about the possibility of preventing conception of most congenital abnormalities. For example, Penrose estimated that avoidance of conception by subnormal parents would not have a large effect on the frequency of mental subnormality in the general population.[1] Nor is there at present any other means of identifying most parents likely to have abnormal children. The conclusion therefore seems inescapable, that the most promising approach to the control of serious conditions which can be neither prevented nor successfully treated is identification during pregnancy and removal by abortion. Having regard for the size and intractability of congenital problems, there can be few more important tasks confronting biomedical research of the laboratory type than the study of amniocentesis and other methods of recognizing abnormal embryos or foetuses in early pregnancy.

This is not to suggest that there should be no further support for other lines of investigation, designed to identify deleterious influences in pregnancy (such as thalidomide or rubella), or to lead to treatment (which has been successful in a few biochemical disorders). Nevertheless within the foreseeable future it would be unwise to expect prevention or treatment to provide a solution of the most formidable congenital problems: mental subnormality and the congenital malformations.

1. Penrose, L. S., *The Biology of Mental Defect* (London: Sidgwick and Jackson Ltd, 1963), p. 288.

MENTAL ILLNESS

Mental illness presents one of the most serious challenges to medical research: first because there is little evidence of success in the past; and second, because with the exception of the form due to an infection (syphilis of the central nervous system), there has been no response to the influences which have brought about the decline of physical (mainly infectious) diseases. But the slow rate of progress has at least the excuse that the problems are inherently difficult; it is a fair guess that if all the Nobel prize-winners of this century had worked in psychiatry, the subject would have advanced only a little less slowly and none of them would have received the prize.

But in what direction should we be looking, having in mind the conclusions in Part One? Broadly there are the same grounds for reservations about a laboratory approach as in the case of physical illness. During man's evolution, natural selection must have restricted the frequency of genetically determined mental illness to a low level. The common diseases such as mental subnormality and the psychoses are not therefore established irreversibly at fertilization, but are due to influences acting on variable genetic material. Operationally the important consideration is not the nature of the genetic component or the balance sheet of nature and nurture; it is the feasibility of identifying and controlling the environmental influences.

In the case of mental subnormality these influences are usually, although by no means invariably, prenatal; in the case of the psychoses and psychoneuroses as a working hypothesis it seems reasonable to believe that they are mainly post-natal. And just as we think of agents entering the nose and mouth as likely to be important in respiratory and digestive diseases, so we should look to behavioural influences as the probable source of most disorders of behaviour.

Unfortunately Freudian psychology, which might have been expected to lead in this direction, from this point of view at least has been a disappointment. Therapeutically it has merely conferred a secular blessing on the practice of confession, and with its emphasis on therapy it has not led to the search for influences which might be modified or removed. What are needed are not so much recollections of how parents treated their children in the distant past as observations on how they treat them in the present.

But it is by no means certain that the conventional approach, even of epidemiological research, will be successful when applied to the study of behaviour. Let us imagine a line drawn from Jesus Christ to Dr Gallup and passing through such eminent investigators of the human condition as Karl Marx, Max Weber, the Webbs, and Dr Kinsey. I think that while there might be differences of opinion about the order of names, it would be generally agreed that from Christ to Gallup the issues become pettier and the scope for research, particularly of a numerical kind, becomes greater. When Christ said 'he that shall findeth his life shall lose it', and La Rochefoucauld 'that it is easier to generalize about mankind than to understand any one man', perceptive people recognize that they were making profound observations on the human condition. Yet their conclusions were not the result of scientific inquiry and, once made, no science was needed to validate them.

The conclusion to be drawn is that the solution, however distant, of a psychiatric problem such as schizophrenia may come, not from treatment of the established disorder by biochemical or other methods, but, as in the case of all other major diseases which have so far been controlled, by removal of influences which have led to the abnormality. If so, the main emphasis of medical research should be on identification of those influences, by careful observation and reflection on the history of schizophrenics and their families, by comparison with non-affected families, and by review of experience of the disease in different populations and sections of populations. This is of course the approach of the epidemiologist; but he will need even more inspiration than in the study of physical illness. In general, he should proceed like Christ rather than Gallup, suspecting the answer before starting to look for it, and using subsequent research to provide an opportunity for his hunches to be proved wrong.

PHYSICAL ILLNESS

Both past experience (of the infections) and theoretical considerations suggest that for the solution of most problems of physical illness, as distinct from measures needed while they remain unsolved, we should be searching for environmental influences which have led to the diseases. The exceptions are conditions determined irreversibly at fertilization: the small number associated with gene or chromosome disorders and the larger number which result from the genetically programmed wearing out of organs at the end of life.

The main restriction on this approach is likely to be in respect of congenital abnormalities, because of the difficulty of identifying and controlling influences which operate during implantation and early embryonic development. Most serious malformations are determined within a few weeks of fertilization when it is difficult, at least on the basis of present knowledge, to imagine effective intervention. It is for this reason that amniocentesis and related procedures are so important.

The success of the approach in post-natal life is evident from the transformation in the health of infants and young people, essentially by improved feeding and modification of the environment in which they live. But until quite recently it was an open question whether the same procedure would succeed with the diseases of middle and late life, many of which were thought to be established at the time of fertilization.

The answer has come from epidemiological investigations of cancer, perhaps the most significant finding in medical research since the discovery that infectious diseases could be prevented by attention to nutrition and hygiene. It is now evident that most cancers are attributable to environmental influences, if we include under this term not only tobacco, refined foods, industrial carcinogens, and the like, but also variation in reproductive behaviour. In the light of this success it is not unreasonably optimistic to believe it is possible that many other residual health problems may be due to influences which might be controlled.

It is not suggested that all these influences will be easy to identify or, when identified, to remove. Chapter 2 referred to some of the difficulties: the influences may be multiple, as in coronary artery disease; or expensive to modify, as in substitution for industrial carcinogens; or intractable for complex biological reasons, as in malaria and schistosomiasis; or they may require changes of behaviour, as in the case of smoking. Nevertheless it is on investigation and control of such influences that hopes for continuing improvement in human health must largely rest.

BEHAVIOUR, ENVIRONMENT, AND NUTRITION

As the major determinants of health, these influences should now have the attention from medical research that their importance merits. In the past the study of personal behaviour in relation to disease was of no more than marginal interest, the discovery of environmental hazards has resulted mainly from fortuitous observations rather than systematic inquiry and knowledge of the relation between malnutrition and infectious disease is based on clinical experience rather than laboratory research.

The research needed is broadly of two kinds. First we require study of influences which are harmful; the investigation of the relation between dietary fibre and intestinal diseases during the past decade is an excellent example of this type of research. Second, when hazards are recognized, there may be formidable problems related to their removal. The outstanding examples are smoking in advanced countries and the rapid growth of population in developing countries. Indeed it is an indication of the change of direction needed in medical research that the most important health problems to be solved today are probably elimination of smoking and, in poor countries, reduction in family size.

QUALITY OF CARE

In Chapter 7 attention was drawn to the importance of the study of three aspects of quality of care: standards, effectiveness, and efficiency. The subject is referred to again, briefly, because this a task for medical research. In the past, the mechanistic approach was partly responsible for acceptance of clinical impressions of the usefulness of a procedure as sufficient grounds for its introduction; in general a new measure was assumed to be effective and safe unless it was shown to be otherwise. Against the background of historical evidence, of a different concept of the origin of disease, and of the sobering results of assessment of some procedures and services in current use, we should start now from a different assumption. It should be recognized that disease problems are rarely solved by therapeutic intervention, that new methods of investigation and treatment are often ineffective and are sometimes unsafe, and that laboratory evidence, however exhaustive, is not a sufficient basis for judgement of the effects of a procedure when applied to man. There is no substitute for clinical trials, which should have a prominent place in any comprehensive research programme. As emphasized in Chapter 7 the aim should be to achieve control, through scientific appraisal of new developments before they are accepted as suitable for general use.

BIOMEDICAL RESEARCH

The proposals outlined above could lead to a change in biomedical research affecting both its aims and its methods. Its primary concern would be to solve health problems by identification of deleterious influences rather than through treatment of established disease, and for this purpose it would rely more heavily on epidemiological than on laboratory methods. At the same time it should be recognized that this would be only a change in emphasis, for there are compelling reasons for continued support of the conventional approach.

1. So long as the deleterious influences are not eliminated, either because they are unrecognized, as in breast cancer, or because we are unable or unwilling to accept their removal, as in the case of road accidents, there will be need for continued treatment of diseases and disabilities which in principle are avoidable. Indeed some of the greatest successes of clinical medicine are in treatment of conditions such as accidents which, ideally, should not occur. This approach must rely largely on laboratory science.

2. Even when the solution of a major health problem is in sight, as was the case with most infections early in this century, personal measures based on laboratory medicine, may make a substantial

contribution in the short and medium term. This was true of tuberculosis and diphtheria.

3. Laboratory investigation may provide an understanding of disease processes which is essential for control of the environment, as illustrated by the hygienic measures which relied on identification of micro-organisms.

4. Among conditions which seem almost intractable, such as those determined at fertilization, there is occasionally scope for effective treatment. Phenylketonuria is an example.

5. While laboratory science, particularly at the molecular level, is unlikely to solve the outstanding health problems in the foreseeable future, it would be a mistake to conclude that it could never do so.

What is needed, therefore, is a judicious placing of bets. For the short and medium term the main investment should be on the approach which has succeeded in the past and, on the basis of present knowledge, seems likely to contribute most in future: identification of influences responsible for disease. However, it would be prudent to have a substantial side-bet on laboratory science, in the knowledge that it will assist with contemporary problems and in the hope that it may contribute in unpredictable ways at some time in the future.

IO

Dream, mirage,
or Nemesis?

In Dostoevsky's novel *The Possessed* there is a hilarious chapter which describes a meeting of provincial liberals who have assembled to hear a message from two prominent radicals. Unfortunately the great men seem less interested in revolution than in brandy and cards, and the conversation becomes trivial, heated, confused, irrelevant to the great issues they have come to hear discussed. Finally the host despairingly begs someone to make a statement, and they proceed to vote on the question whether they are a meeting in some formal sense, or merely a group of friends who have met to celebrate a name-day.

In medicine also there is confusion but, by contrast, no lack of statements; indeed there is a surfeit of them. Unfortunately for the earnest seeker after truth they are by no means consistent and some are frankly contradictory. (One is reminded of the opening paragraph of *A Tale of Two Cities*: 'It was the best of times, it was the worst of times . . .'). So we are told on the one hand that medical science has already achieved miracles and that if we will only provide the resources and have a little patience it will shortly solve all our problems, and on the other that an exact evaluation of twentieth-century medicine would do much to restore nineteenth-century faith in prayer. It is said that many countries already enjoy a high standard of health which will soon be raised further, and, on the contrary, that with changing conditions of life disease problems must also be expected to change and the goal of improved health is largely illusory. The doctor is described as a man of principle devoted to the advancement of science and the welfare of his patients, and as a charlatan who can be counted on to look after nothing but his own interests.

Some of the scepticism is perhaps no more than good-natured banter of the kind to which the professions seem particularly

157

exposed; certainly no worse than things that are said about clergy-
men and a good deal kinder than many reflections on the work
of lawyers. But whatever the motivation in the past there is undoubtedly a new note of severity in contemporary criticism; the
critics, or at least some of them, mean what they say. Here, for
example, are the observations of Nancy Mitford on the work of
doctors at the time of Louis XIV and today.

The fashionable doctors . . . stood as they do now, in admiration of their own
science. As now, they talked as if illness and death were mastered. Molière has
presented that sort of doctor once and for all; a consultation of big-wigs is ever
a scene from one of his plays. The learned, magic, meaningless words, the grave
looks at each other, the artful hesitation between one worthless formula and
another—all are there. In those days, terrifying in black robes and bonnets they
bled the patient; now terrifying in white robes and masks they pump blood
into him. The result is the same; the strong live; the weak, after much suffering
and expense, both of spirit and money, die.[1]

Such criticisms should be taken seriously, and for a number of
reasons. In the first place, there is a good deal of truth in the allega-
tions. Doctors have always tended to overestimate the effectiveness of their intervention and to underestimate the risks, whether
removing large quantities of blood, under mistaken notions of
the blood volume, in the treatment of yellow fever in the eighteenth century, or exposing patients to dangerous levels of radia-
tion, of whose effects they were unaware, when screening for
breast cancer in the twentieth. There was and is still a good deal
of unjustified complacency about the extent of understanding of
disease and of ability to control it, for example, in the assumptions
that malaria and schistosomiasis will soon be eradicated or that
there is little more to fear from airborne infections. And patients
have been and continue to be exposed to pain and injury from
misguided attempts to do them good. Suffering is only marginally
more tolerable when inflicted with the best intentions, and the
death of Charles II under treatment by his doctors was much more
cruel than that of his father at the hands of his executioner.
Indeed the history of treatment of illness in the aristocracy,[2] who
were able to obtain the 'best' medical care, suggests that Francis

1. Mitford, N., *The Sun King* (London: Sphere Books Ltd, 1969), p. 141.
2. Excellently recorded for the French Court in the Memoirs of Saint-Simon.

Galton was generous in his conclusion that there is a considerable difference between a good doctor and a bad one, but hardly any difference between a good doctor and none at all.

A second reason for reappraisal of the role of doctors is the more independent line now taken by other health professionals. In some respects this is less a result of a fresh assessment of the needs of patients than an expression of the spirit of our times, when notions of equality and freedom are applied in all circumstances, even to the relation between parents and children. But it is also true that nurses, social workers, hygienists, and others have come to believe that they can often function just as effectively without the advice, and much more happily without the supervision of the doctor.

There is also a change in public attitudes to medicine, less evident in Britain than in the United States. In that country the image of the doctor as a devoted healer has been shaken by the resistance of professional organizations to the introduction of publicly financed and administered health services, and by the unwillingness of doctors to practice in areas which they find unattractive: even, in some cases, where patients are able to meet the costs of private medical care. To many people doctors seem less concerned about the welfare of patients than about their own convenience and standard of living. In such circumstances insistence on the delicacy of the doctor–patient relationship by the physician seems an anomaly, equivalent to the suggestion that the privacy of the confessional is intended to protect, not the sinner but the priest.

As noted in an earlier chapter, these reactions to the doctor's position have been muted to some extent by the belief that his role is critical for the health of patients. When it becomes generally known, as surely it will, that the determinants of health are largely outside the medical care system, the questions are likely to become even more insistent. If we are neither cured when we are ill nor well cared for when we are disabled, what is the role of medicine in which so much has been invested, in hope and resources?

I have put the question in the provocative form in which it may be asked, indeed in which it has already been asked by some who have lost faith in the work of doctors. But if the question is overstated so too are likely to be the answers. From the belief that medicine can do everything, opinion is in danger of swinging to the equally untenable conclusion that it can do little or nothing. It is therefore important for the public as well as for the profession itself, that the medical role should be reconsidered, fairly and objectively, taking account of both its achievements in the past and its probable contributions in the foreseeable future.

In examining the medical role I shall refer to four books which raise many of the important issues. They are *The Lives of a Cell*,[1] *Dreams, Genes and Realities*,[2] *The Mirage of Health*,[3] and *Medical Nemesis*.[4]

DREAM

Perhaps the most commonly held opinion is that medicine has already solved many disease problems, and if it is not yet in sight of a solution of all that remain, it is unquestionably on the right lines. There is also the modified view that the dream has faded, that formerly there were great achievements, but what remains is much less impressive, the 'degenerate remnant of something immense in the past'.[5] On the first interpretation there is little need for a change of direction, but on the second a reappraisal of the medical role is clearly required.

The more cheerful conclusion was expressed with due caution by Thomas in terms which would probably be acceptable to most biomedical scientists. He suggested that 'the great contemporary achievement of modern medicine is the technology for controlling and preventing bacterial infection', and he cited as examples 'immunisation against diphtheria, pertussis (and the childhood virus diseases) and the contemporary use of antibiotics and chemo-therapy for bacterial infections' such as syphilis and tuberculosis. Thomas recognized the limitations of medical measures: 'For all

1. Thomas, L., *The Lives of a Cell* (Toronto, New York, London: Bantam Books Inc., 1975).
2. Burnet, Sir Macfarlane, *Genes, Dreams and Realities* (Aylesbury, Bucks: Medical and Technical Publishing Co. Ltd, 1971).
3. Dubos, R., *The Mirage of Health* (London: George Allen and Unwin Ltd, 1960).
4. Illich, I., *Medical Nemesis* (London: Calder and Boyars Ltd, 1975).
5. Auden, W. H., *Poems* (London: Faber and Faber Ltd, 1934), p. 64. (Auden's version of Chekhov's 'the shrinking remannt of something which was once enormous'.)

the new knowledge, we still have formidable diseases, still unsolved, lacking satisfactory explanation, lacking satisfactory treatment'; and 'In real life, the biomedical sciences have not yet reached the stage of any kind of general applicability to disease mechanisms'. Significantly, he saw a parallel with the physical sciences of the early twentieth century, 'booming along into new territory, but without an equivalent for the engineering of the time'. However he doubted whether the further development of applied science in medicine can be hurried, and suggested that 'the greatest part of the important biomedical research waiting to be done is in the class of basic science'.[1]

The grounds for one's reservations about this interpretation were discussed in previous chapters and need not be repeated at length. But briefly, with the possible exception of diphtheria, mortality from the common infections (tuberculosis, pneumonia, scarlet fever, measles, pertussis, etc.) had declined to quite a low level before effective immunization, antibiotics, and chemotherapy became available. The largest contribution of biomedical science was the extension of hygienic measures made possible by understanding of disease and identification of micro-organisms. Control of the infections resulted mainly from modification of the conditions under which they occurred, and there are theoretical as well as historical reasons for believing that the same approach is the most promising for an attack on the disease problems that remain.

Very different views were expressed by a distinguished microbiologist in *Dreams, Genes and Realities*. Burnet suggested 'that future historians may speak of an age of scientific discovery that started with Galileo in 1586 and ended something less than four hundred years later'. He implied that laboratory research made a large contribution in the past, but it cannot be expected to do so in future, when the most important challenges will be the so-called 'intrinsic' types of disease and disability (cancer, old-age, and auto-immune disease), diseases of civilization (lung cancer, road accidents, alcoholism, drug addiction, etc.), and the general problems of society which impinge on health: limitation of population growth, disarmament, and control of the environment. In

1. Thomas, L., *The Lives of a Cell.*

161

solving such problems laboratory medicine has little to offer, and pride of place in biology is now held by the observational sciences, ecology and ethology, 'because of their rather direct bearing on contemporary human problems'.[1]

Broadly, Burnet's views seem closer to those of Thomas in respect of the past and to those expressed in this book in respect of the future. Although he recognized that 'The accelerating increase of human populations since the eighteenth century has depended mainly on two factors, an increase in the amount of food available and the development, incidentally or deliberately, of ways of diminishing infectious disease', he suggested that specific measures of prevention (DDT and other potent insecticides), immunization, and treatment 'have changed a steady population increase into an explosion'. While this may be true (particularly of DDT and insecticides) in developing countries today, it is not accurate for the developed countries in the past three centuries, when the decline of mortality and growth of population were essentially independent of specific measures. The interpretation, therefore, somewhat overstates the contribution of laboratory medicine in the past; it may also understate its value in the future: for example, it is by no means unlikely that amniocentesis and related measures discovered mainly by laboratory research will make it possible to recognize and eliminate many serious abnormalities before birth. But the general conclusions, that most diseases and disabilities determined at fertilization will remain intractable, and that abnormalities attributable to conditions of life will be controlled by modification of those conditions rather than through laboratory investigation, seem unexceptionable. However, an epidemiologist is unlikely to be persuaded that the interest and the usefulness of the tasks confronting the research worker no longer coincide.

MIRAGE

One of the most interesting ideas related to the medical role is the notion that the goal of improved health is to some extent illusory, a mirage which inspires and attracts but will continue to elude us, however diligently we seek it. This concept was out-

1. Burnet, Sir Macfarlane, *Genes, Dreams and Realities*.

lined by Dubos in *The Mirage of Health*,[1] and stated explicitly in a later book:

> It is a dangerous error to believe that disease and suffering can be wiped out altogether by raising still further the standards of living, increasing our mastery of the environment, and developing new therapeutic procedures. The less pleasant reality is that, since the world is ever changing, each period and each type of civilisation will continue to have its burden of diseases created by the unavoidable failure of biological and social adaptation to counter new environmental threads.[2]

This interpretation seems consistent with man's history until the last three centuries. During most of its existence he lived as a nomad, dependent on fortuitous food sources and, like other animals in their natural habitats, subject to rigorous natural selection which kept disease at a low frequency. With small populations at low densities infectious diseases as we have known them in the historical period were not a serious problem, and illness and early death were determined by the primitive conditions of life: food shortage, homicide, accidents, and predation.

The first Agricultural Revolution ten thousand years ago led to profound changes. A settled way of life and domestication of plants and animals increased food supplies and resulted in population growth. The aggregation of large populations created the conditions needed for the propagation and transmission of microorganisms, particularly those that were air-, water-, and food-borne. However, with unrestricted growth of population food supplies became again marginal, so that lack of food was once more an important source of ill-health. But there was this difference from the earlier period, that infectious diseases had become the predominant cause of sickness and death.

To this point, roughly to 1700, experience seems entirely consistent with the view that as conditions of life change we move from one set of health problems to another: 'We owe God a death. He that dies this year is quit for the next.'[3] But is the interpretation equally valid when applied to the last three centuries,

---

1. Dubos, R., *The Mirage of Health*.
2. Dubos, R., *Man, Medicine, and Environment* (London: Pall Mall Press, 1968), p. 85.
3. *Henry IV, Part II.*

and what is even more important: does it suggest that there are strict limits to the health goals that can be reached in future?

Perhaps the first point which should be made is that it is a very restricted view of life which can be obtained by inspection of death certificates. Everyone must die, but it makes a great difference to health whether the deaths are in early, middle, or late life. The changes since 1700 resulted in a large increase in expectation of life, reflected in a transfer of deaths from early to late life. The transformation of causes of sickness and death during the past three centuries cannot therefore be described accurately as the exchange of one set of health problems for another.

In developing countries today the predominant infectious diseases can also be dealt with by measures which do not of themselves create health problems of another kind. However it is a short step from sufficient food to a surfeit, and in the developed world a new set of problems has appeared, essentially those associated with the changes of behaviour which are possible in an affluent society. Are these problems which appear after the decline of the infections likely to be solved without creating new ones?

The residual problems vary greatly in their character. Those determined at fertilization or by prenatal influences (see Chapter 2) have been little affected by recent changes, and are probably neither more nor less tractable than they were before. Those due to lack of food or environmental hazards can be resolved by an extension of measures which have been successful hitherto, although this will require strict control of new risks, particularly those associated with industrial processes and medical procedures. The possibility that one group of health problems has been exchanged for another arises most seriously in relation to the diseases of affluence. They appear to be due largely to a departure from conditions of life under which man evolved, and the question is whether a return to those conditions in order to prevent them is feasible.

In some cases there is no obvious reason why it should not be. Both health and quality of life are improved by taking exercise, avoiding tobacco and other drugs, and limiting consumption of alcohol and food. As these are now the main determinants of health it is hard to believe that society will not wish to create conditions under which such practices are encouraged. In many ways the problems are epitomized by smoking, where the serious damage to the health of large numbers of people has to be weighed against the commercial and other interests which will suffer if smoking is reduced and finally stopped.

A problem which differs only in degree is that of traffic accidents. It is unlikely that society will accept elimination of motor vehicles, although their limitation and stricter control will be inevitable, not only for health reasons. What does seem unacceptable is a high level of accidents due to drinking and driving, and stringent measures have already been introduced, for example in Sweden.

A class of health problems for which it is perhaps most difficult to see a possible solution are those related to changes in reproductive behaviour. The infections due to promiscuity can conceivably be controlled by preventive measures or treatment; but it is possible that the profound changes in reproduction associated with the fall of the birth-rate since the nineteenth century have contributed to the prevalence of breast cancer and other diseases of the reproductive system. If so, these abnormalities truly represent the problem to which Dubos referred, the appearance of new diseases as a consequence of the conditions which led to the decline of the old ones. Society may very well return to some of our ancestral practices, for example by increasing exercise, reducing fat consumption, and replacing refined flour by whole meal. It would find it much more difficult to accept early and frequent pregnancies, should it be shown that these are the changes needed to reduce the frequency of cancer of the breast.

In conclusion: While it is true that disease and suffering cannot be wiped out, particularly those forms determined at fertilization or by prenatal influences, experience of the past three centuries shows that it is possible to achieve an enormous improvement in health by modification of post-natal influences. Of the three which have been most effective, increased food supplies, control of hazards, and limitation of numbers, only the last may be associated with a new set of disease problems, brought about by the change in reproductive practice. However the wealth which led to the improvement of nutrition and hygiene has made it possible

165

to depart radically from the conditions under which man evolved, by over-eating, under-exercising, smoking, and the like. Whether future progress in health will be restricted by these changes will depend on whether men are prepared to modify their life styles and follow the principles by which some dissenting minorities have lived for centuries. Perhaps the ideal to which we should aspire is that of the Quaker of moderate but firm convictions, who believes that it is permissible, even desirable to have wealth so long as it is not abused. Shaw touched on the same point in the Preface to *Man and Superman* when he wrote: 'Do not waste your time on Social Questions. What is the matter with the poor is Poverty. What is the matter with the rich is Uselessness.' It has taken hundreds of thousands of years to remove the ill-health associated with poverty, and we should not be surprised if it takes a little time to remove that which is associated with wealth. But there is no reason for despondency on the grounds that we have merely exchanged one set of health problems for another.

NEMESIS

A third suggestion to be considered is that the role of medicine is essentially sinister. It should not surprise us, for it has been made before; but in terms so benign that the offence of what was said was quite removed by the manner of saying it. People, including medical people, were more amused than provoked when Shaw described the medical service as a murderous absurdity, and referred to the physician as, among other things, a credulous imposter, petulant scientific coxcomb, and parasite on disease. In Illich's *Medical Nemesis* the conclusions are much the same but the tone is different; with passion and without humour he described the medical role as a threat, to society as well as patients, that can only be removed by a public unfrocking of the offending practitioners.[1]

The grounds for this proposal are said to be threefold: medicine does more harm than good; it breeds demands for its services and supports features of society which generate ill health; most seriously, it diminishes the capacity of the individual to deal with

1. Illich, I., *Medical Nemesis.*

his own health problems and to face suffering and death. Let us consider them in turn.

1. The assertion that 'a professional and physician-based health care system . . . must produce clinical damages which outweigh its practical benefits' is rather like a statement that there is more evil than good in the world. There may be; but there is no means of proving or disproving it, and in both the medical and the celestial balance sheets the decision must turn on definitions and value judgements. My own impression, for what it is worth, is that if the term medicine is taken to include the whole enterprise —nutritional, hygienic, and behavioural as well as therapeutic— there is little doubt that the balance is strongly in medicine's favour. If it is restricted to clinical services, the answer varies from place to place and from physician to physician. Certainly there are countries where one would not like to be ill, and there are doctors in all countries by whom one would prefer not to be treated. But there are others to whom one would go unhesitatingly with a disease problem, confident that the advice would be sound and the treatment, if required, beneficial and never harmful. The conclusion that clinical damages *must* outweigh the benefits is mistaken, and if they sometimes do the answer is to make the services better rather than to blow them up. It is perhaps worth noting that Illich was misinformed about the value of some of the procedures to which he refers: the decline of pneumonia is not attributable mainly to sulphonamides and antibiotics; although treatment of typhoid is effective the disease cannot be said to be cured quite easily; vaccines have contributed little to the decline of deaths from whooping cough and measles; the effect of replacement therapy on diabetes is not only in the short run; the value of vaginal smears in intervention for cervical cancer has not been proved; and the effectiveness of drug treatment of high blood pressure is not restricted to patients with malignant hypertension. There are some advantages in having medical experience when assessing medical procedures.

2. It is well recognized that the demand for clinical services increases with their availability; just as some children can occupy the attention of as many adults as are prepared to wait on them,

some patients appear to require the services of as many doctors as can be persuaded to see them. But the conclusion that on this account physician services as we know them should cease, is rather like the suggestion that because some people over-eat there should be no more baking of bread. Of course there is a problem of restricting demand for a wide range of consumer services, but it will not be solved simply by bringing them to an end.

It is more difficult to come to grips with the second point under the same heading: that health policies reinforce an industrial organization which generates ill health. Like another passionate critic of health services (Enoch Powell), Illich gives an impression of lucidity while sometimes leaving one in doubt about the precise meaning of what he is saying. It is not obvious that medical intervention contributes to two of the main determinants of ill health—lack of food and environmental hazards; and belief in the value of treatment probably has little effect on the predominant behavioural influences—for example, the mistaken idea that doctors can cure cancer of the lung and chronic bronchitis is not in the mind of the adolescent when he begins smoking. Illich refers in the same context to a different point: the survival of increasing numbers of defectives who require institutional care. Only a very small part of this problem is attributable to misguided medical intervention, such as surgical treatment of children seriously handicapped by spina bifida; the large majority of mentally retarded people now survive, not because of specific medical measures, but because society is unwilling to withhold from them the basic necessities of life. For many of us the solution of the problem of the congenitally handicapped, if and when there is one, lies not in denial of humane care, but in avoidance of their conception or birth.

3. Illich seems to attach most importance to his third point: that medical services reduce the capacity of the individual to care for himself and to face suffering and death. He appears to believe that medical procedures fall broadly into two classes: those that are cheap, effective, and simple, so that the patient could apply them himself; and those that are expensive, complicated, and useless, so that little would be lost if they were abandoned. In this reading

there would be only occasional need for 'specialized healers', although they presumably would have to advise patients from time to time whether their services were necessary: like the doctor in Mary Baker Eddy's biography, called to see a sick Christian Scientist who was no better after several hours of intensive prayer, and told that he was not to do anything, but merely to ascertain what should be prayed for.

There are many things people should do for their health but they are not those that Illich has chiefly in mind. I believe they should recognize that they are healthy and live in such a way that they remain so; he emphasizes their frailty, and would like them to take over their treatment and, when this fails, bear with their suffering.

The notion that the application of effective treatment is usually simple is mistaken. Streptomycin, one of the most valuable therapeutic agents, is easily administered; but it is necessary first to be sure that the patient has tuberculosis and that is not a simple matter. Antibiotics are commonly misused by doctors in treatment of respiratory diseases; they are even more likely to be abused by the public who can hardly be expected to distinguish clearly between viral and bacterial infections. Some of the most useful procedures, such as treatment of accidents, dental conditions, and unpredictable obstetric emergencies, require both specialized equipment and professional skill. But more generally, the gross abuse of drugs already available to the public gives no ground for confidence that if medical control (by no means wholly effective) were withdrawn all would be well; indeed it is probable that the harm which results from self-administered sedatives, analgesics, tranquillizers, etc., not to mention tobacco, alcohol, and opiates is already far greater than that caused by medical intervention.

The most complex matter is the attitude to pain and suffering which is not only, or mainly, a health-related question. The ideas about suffering are very ancient: Epicurus maintained that a man could be happy on the rack and wrote on the day of his death: 'On this truly happy day of my life, as I am on the point of death, I write this to you. The diseases of my bladder and stomach are pursuing their course, lacking nothing of their usual severity:

but against all this is the joy in my heart at the recollection of my conversations with you.' The Stoics taught endurance rather than hope; cruelty and injustice should not be resented since they provide excellent opportunities for the practice of virtue, and medical men are unnecessary because illness is not an evil. 'I must die. But must I die groaning?' Epictetus asked, and he held that happiness resulted from 'the sense that your affairs depend on no one'. Related ideas are to be found in St Augustine and Tolstoy, both of whom were obsessed by a sense of sin, original and self-engendered, which could be expurgated only by suffering. The significance of misery was central to Pascal's thought: 'La connaissance de Dieu sans celle de notre misère fait l'orgueil; la connaissance de notre misère sans celle de Jésus-Christ fait le désespoir.' Kierkegaard wrote with satisfaction: 'The human race has in the course of generations become ever more insignificant', and he and others have implied that the world would be the poorer if pain and suffering were eliminated.

There are at least three ideas interwoven in these reflections: pain and misery are inescapable (Pascal); they are rewarding (St Augustine and Tolstoy); and one should prepare to face them (Epicurus and Epictetus). If these views are accepted there is obviously little to be said for employing professional healers whose task is to relieve distress.

When Pascal wrote of 'notre misère' he referred to mental as well as physical suffering; in the present context it will be sufficiently ambitious to restrict attention to the latter. The idea that pain and suffering are inevitable is I think mistaken: it was probably true, or very nearly so, for most of man's life on earth; but with the provision of sufficient food and control of hazards in the past few centuries, many people have completed their lives without severe or prolonged physical discomfort. It is also true that medicine can contribute largely to the relief of such suffering when it occurs, and even saints and reformed sinners would accept anaesthesia for removal of an impacted third molar, and surgical intervention for treatment of a perforated peptic ulcer or obstructed labour.

The conclusion that physical suffering is not inevitable and can often be relieved when it occurs does not of course meet the objection that pain is rewarding and should be accepted, even sought rather than resisted. Such ideas usually come from people of exceptional sensitivity and imagination who should be careful about prescribing for others who are less gifted or less afflicted than themselves. A man may say paradoxically: I find life a misery yet dread the prospect of death; I can come to terms with existence only if I resign myself to pain and suffering. But except on religious grounds, which can be accepted or rejected, he should not pass the same harsh sentence on other people, I suspect the large majority, who do not share his anguish, and find severe and prolonged suffering, like severe and prolonged poverty, degrading rather than elevating. Moreover response to distress is not un-related to the background and condition of the individual who bears it; it is one thing to give up wealth, like Francis of Assisi, and quite another never to have had it. After a period of de-bauchery, repentance at Yasnaya Polyana must have been more refreshing for its master than for one of his servants, and the down-and-outness of an Old Etonian who subsequently put his experience into a book[1] was very different from that of a peasant who fled from rural poverty in East Bengal to urban squalor on the streets of Calcutta. It would be unfortunate if the prescription for bearing the ills of the flesh were written by those who bear mainly the ills of the mind, for there are many more suffering peasants than there are Tolstoys and Orwells.

Accommodation to life's minor trials is another matter. An obstetrician at the hospital where I trained as a medical student used to tell of a Spanish town which went into mourning when the blinds were drawn at the great house to indicate that its mistress was having her period. There is something to be said for the view that people should not thrust their problems unreasonably on others, for although Freud's teaching is appropriate to great suffering, the advice of Moody and Sankey—'Go bury thy sorrow, the world hath its share'—is more in keeping with the requirements of everyday life.

1. Orwell, G., *Down and Out in Paris and London* (London: Secker and War-burg, 1949).

THE MEDICAL ROLE

Having touched in the preceding pages on various ideas related to the medical role, I must now try to bring them together in a more coherent form. Before doing so, however, it will be desirable to remove one or two possible sources of misunderstanding.

First, the aim of health services. We know from personal experience that the feeling of well-being, sometimes referred to as positive health, is something more than the absence of recognizable disease and disability, and it is tempting to define objectives, as the World Health Organization has defined them, in terms which recognize this.[1] However there are at least two objections to so broad a definition: one, that positive health cannot be measured accurately, so that success or failure in achieving it can only be judged subjectively; the other, that since many influences, personal, religious, educational, and economic as well as medical, contribute to a state of well-being, the concept goes far beyond the responsibilities of health services. I shall therefore define the aim more modestly as the prevention of sickness and premature death and the care of the sick and disabled. In these terms the task of medicine is not to create happiness, but so far as possible to remove a major source of unhappiness, that which results from illness and early death.

At the outset also I should like to sidestep the trade union disputes which arise over the role of doctor in relation to that of other health workers. As noted in an earlier chapter these roles are changing, and at some future time the respective trainings and responsibilities of the physician and nurse in primary care, and of the physician and social worker in care of the subnormal, may be quite different from those which exist today. When commenting on the medical role I am therefore referring to the work done by doctors and others concerned with 'prevention of sickness and premature death and care of the sick and disabled', and I am not specifying or implying any unique role for the physician. My concern is with the work to be done rather than with who should do it.

1. In the constitution of the World Health Organization health was defined as a 'state of complete physical, mental and social well-being and not merely the absence of disease or infirmity'.

The role of medicine

In the light of the interpretation of disease discussed in previous chapters I suggest that the role of medicine should be conceived as follows: To assist us to come safely into the world and comfortably out of it, and during life to protect the well and care for the sick and disabled.

SAFELY INTO THE WORLD

Since I shall certainly be told that we can come into the world (and out of it) without medical assistance, I have taken care to suggest for medicine only a supplementary role. But under it I am referring to much more than the act of delivery itself: to prevention of the birth of the seriously abnormal, and to limitation of the number of births, as well as to the safeguarding of normal pregnancy and labour.

I do not think medicine has anything to contribute in relation to such questionable and technically remote objectives as selection of parents in order to improve the human race. But it is reasonable to identify parents whose likelihood of having a seriously abnormal birth can be specified—for example to tell those who have had a child with a malformation of the heart or central nervous system that the risk of malformation in a later birth is increased above the average risk, but is still relatively low. It would be even better if it were possible to specify the risk of congenital abnormalities for parents who have not previously had an abnormal child; but since the common ones are probably determined by intra-uterine conditions, this is not at present a very promising objective.

Identification of deleterious influences during pregnancy is equally important, and perhaps equally difficult. Nevertheless it is possible that other agents such as thalidomide and rubella will be discovered, and if they are external to the uterus they may be easily removed. Influences arising within the uterus are much more difficult to recognize and control.

On the basis of present knowledge, or of any probable extension of it, neither of these approaches—identification of parents likely to have abnormal births or of deleterious influences during pregnancy which can be removed—offers much prospect of control of most serious congenital conditions. It is for this reason that in the discussion of research (Chapter 9) so much importance was attached to recognition of the abnormal foetus in early pregnancy when it can be aborted.

Doctors have no more and no less right than other people to define the limits of population growth; but the limits having been defined they have a role in the prevention of conception and termination of pregnancy, unless, as Illich suggests, abortion is to be managed on a do-it-yourself basis.[1] In making this proposal he underestimates the technical difficulties, particularly the risk of infection and of later complications.

Clear thinking is needed about the contribution of medicine to the conduct of normal pregnancy and labour. It is quite true that the large majority of people have come into the world without professional assistance, but the mortality of mothers and children was very high until the present century. It is also true that mortality can be reduced dramatically by relatively simple measures, particularly in literate populations which enjoy a high standard of living. In most developed countries maternal mortality is now very low and perinatal and infant mortality are both about 20 (per 1,000). But the difference between low rates and the lowest rates is determined by the handling of occasional unforeseen emergencies which require facilities and skill of the kind available in hospitals. A society which wishes to get the best results will therefore need to provide simple care for all pregnancies with more sophisticated measures in reserve for the unpredictable complications.

PROTECTION OF THE WELL

The conclusion which I hope emerges from the preceding chapters is that the improvement in health hitherto has been due predominantly to protection of people born free of congenital disabilities, and that it is to the same approach that we must look mainly for the solution of the residual problems of the common diseases. Most of those who are born well will remain well, apart from minor morbidity, at least until late life, if they have enough to eat, if they are not exposed to serious hazards, and if they do not injure themselves by unwise behaviour, particularly by

1. Illich, I., *Medical Nemesis.*

174

departing radically from the fundamental conditions under which man evolved.

What part has medicine to play in achieving these objectives? First, since doctors are concerned more comprehensively with human health than any other professional group, they should make it their business to know and to make known, the relative importance of the major influences. Second, the medical contribution in the fields of nutrition and environmental health, where the measures are essentially non-personal, should be in the hands of specialists, who need to be attracted to those subjects as undergraduates and trained in them as graduates. The responsibility which falls on doctors who provide personal care is that of influencing their patients' behaviour in relation to their health. Having regard for the determinants of health a doctor can say to himself quite accurately: In pursuit of the major objectives of preventing sickness and premature death, I can often do more for my patients, particularly young patients, by persuading them to modify their habits than by any treatment that can be offered. The scope for this approach will be even greater when more is known about the common diseases, particularly in the field of mental health where investigation of the major influences has scarcely begun.

CARE OF THE SICK AND DISABLED
Under this heading I include all aspects of care: investigation and treatment of acute illness as well as rehabilitation and prolonged care.

Until the present time the emphasis on medicine has been on only a part of this task, on the kind of work done in acute hospitals: investigation of disease, treatment of acute illness or of acute phases of chronic disease, and treatment of some non-acute conditions (such as hernias, piles, and varicose veins).

At first sight it is not easy to see what determines these interests and excludes others; for example, there is less concern with acute illness in the severely handicapped (the congenitally malformed, the mentally ill, the subnormal, and the very old). Since the eighteenth century the administrations and staffs of general hospitals would have said that they took patients who could make the best use of their resources; but this is not a convincing explanation, since some are admitted who derive little or no benefit, while others are excluded who could be helped. I suggest that there are at least three determinants of the admissions policies of acute hospitals which both reflect and influence the interests of their staffs: they prefer patients who are acutely ill, who are not permanently handicapped, and who provide scope for the current range of investigative and therapeutic procedures. At the present time, with the enormous growth of technology the last is possibly the main determinant; even mongols are occasionally admitted now that they have been shown to have interesting chromosomes.

It is, I believe, a fair criticism of the selective medical interests, that they lead to the neglect of some patients, indeed of the major- ity, and to concern with only a limited part of the needs of those who are helped. But the omissions had this justification, that the work in the acute phase of illness was thought to be critical and largely responsible for the modern improvement in health.

This assumption was mistaken. The treatment of established disease, although important for patients, does not usually restore them to a life of normal duration and quality; and the modern improvement in health was due to prevention of disease rather than to treatment after it occurred.

The conclusion to be drawn is not that the work of the acute hospital can be dispensed with, but that it does not justify so large a proportion of the available resources, or the relative neglect of the majority of hospital patients who are not admitted. Three things are needed: (*a*) a critical appraisal of the effectiveness and efficiency of procedures already in use or to be brought into use; (*b*) recognition that investigation and treatment of the acute episode does not usually change the underlying condition, and that the patient needs advice and care throughout his illness; (*c*) a reshaping of hospitals which removes the arbitrary divisions between the patients in acute, mental, chronic, and mental sub- normality hospitals.

I have discussed the approach to effectiveness and efficiency in Chapter 7. On the second point, treatment of patients, in these days usually elderly patients, in acute episodes of heart disease, cancer, pneumonia, etc., is not a sufficient basis for the main work of a hospital, still less for a concept of the essence of the medical task. This service may be vital to the patients concerned, but it often fails to meet their requirements in the later stages of the illness, or in the months and years which follow when they are no longer in the acute phase. I have written elsewhere at length on the third point, about the origins and consequences of the separation of acute from mental and other hospitals.[1] In the present context all that need be added is that this division has no justification in the different contributions the hospitals are making to the care of the sick and disabled.

COMFORTABLY OUT OF THE WORLD

I refer here not only to terminal care in the period immediately before death, but also to the assistance of patients who may be disabled for months or years before their final illness. Although elderly patients with prolonged incapacity are seen frequently in general practice and in hospital, a large majority of people complete their lives without chronic disease or disability.

The health and related social services need to make much better provision for chronic and terminal care. Both have been relatively neglected, partly because the work is unattractive to many doctors, but also because it is considered less important than investigation and treatment of acute illness. The elderly patient and his relatives cannot be expected to see it in this way. The diagnosis of untreatable cancer (for example) is necessary, but it meets only a small fragment of the patients' needs in the months or years which follow. And although most people end their lives without a period of incapacity, many welcome medical attention in their last illness. Their relatives almost invariably do.

Some centres are concerned with terminal care, and a few devote themselves entirely to patients who face extreme physical and mental distress in their last illness. In effect they are saying: Give us the worst that can happen, and we will show that when professional skill is combined with humane care, the last days of life can be made tolerable, even cheerful, for the most afflicted people. Their work is beyond praise; but it should be taken as an

1. McKeown, T., *Medicine in Modern Society* (London: George Allen and Unwin Ltd, 1965).

example rather than a model, for the size and character of the problem is such that it cannot be divorced from the rest of medical care. Doctors need to regard prolonged and terminal care as an important and rewarding part of their task which should not be transferred to other people or to special institutions. For the patient and relatives the medical contribution to the end of life is as significant as attempts made at an earlier stage to protect or prolong it.

CONCLUSIONS

In the broadest terms, the medical role is in three areas: prevention of disease by personal and non-personal measures; care of the sick who provide scope, or more accurately, under existing services, while they provide scope, for investigation and treatment; and care of the sick who are not thought to require active intervention. Medical interest and resources are focused on the second area and, to a lesser extent, on personal prevention by immunization; the other responsibilities are relatively neglected.

The immediate determinant of the traditional range of interests is the patient's demand for acute care and the physician's wish to provide it. But the approach rests also on a conceptual model, on the belief that health depends primarily on personal intervention, based on understanding of the structure and function of the body and of the disease processes which affect it.

This concept is not in accord with past experience (Chapter 6). The improvement of health during the past three centuries was due essentially to provision of food, protection from hazards, and limitation of numbers; medical science and services made an important contribution to the control of hazards but only a limited one through immunization and therapy.

A theoretical assessment of the determinants of human health (Chapter 2) suggests that the same influences are likely to be effective in future; but there is this difference, that in developed countries personal behaviour (in relation to diet, exercise, tobacco, alcohol, drugs, etc.) is now even more important than provision of food and control of hazards. According to this interpretation few diseases, except for an ill-defined group at the end of life, are determined irreversibly at fertilization; most congenital abnormalities are probably due to intra-uterine conditions operating during implantation and early embryonic development; and most other common diseases are due to post-natal influences. Prenatal determinants are likely to be difficult to identify and control; those which are post-natal vary widely, from some which are simple and tractable (as in the case of many infections) to others which are complex and difficult (for various reasons) to remove. Nevertheless it is on recognition of such post-natal influences that hopes for a solution of the problems of the common diseases, both physical and mental, chiefly rest.

Nothing in these conclusions suggests that the traditional lines of biomedical research are useless and should be brought to an end. On the contrary, they have contributed greatly, by extending the scope and precision of hygienic measures, to a more limited extent by immunization and therapy, but above all, by providing an understanding of the body and its diseases on which the security of effective measures, originally largely intuitive, now substantially rests. However there is need for a shift in the balance of effort, from laboratory research to epidemiology, in recognition that improvement in health is likely to come in future, as in the past, from modification of the conditions which lead to disease, rather than from intervention in the mechanism of disease after it has occurred.

In health services the provision of acute care will continue, needless to say, for it is a response to what the patient usually considers to be his most urgent need. But this service does not justify the predominant place it has occupied until now in medical thought and practice. It is sometimes extremely effective, particularly in treatment of conditions such as accidents which, ideally, should not occur; but often it is ineffective, or merely tides the patient over a short illness, leaving the underlying disease condition and prognosis essentially unchanged. The limitations of the traditional concept of the medical role would have been recognized much earlier, if health had not been transformed in the past three centuries by other influences.

What is needed is an adjustment in the balance of interest and resources between the three main areas of service referred to above. It is essential to give sufficient attention to the personal and non-personal influences which are the major determinants of

179

e p. 172

health: to food and the environment, which will be mainly in the hands of specialists, and to personal behaviour, which should be the concern of every practising doctor. These interests should no longer be peripheral to the medical role, in the way that health education, nutrition, and environmental medicine have been peripheral hitherto. In the field of personal care, the making of a diagnosis and the provision of acute care should be regarded as no more than the beginning of a responsibility which will continue so long as the patient is unwell; and the arbitrary and largely artificial distinctions between different types of patients (acute, chronic, mental, subnormal, etc.) should end.